CASSELL'S DIRECTORY OF

Plants for Family Gardens

CASSELL'S DIRECTORY OF

Plants for Family Gardens

EVERYTHING YOU NEED TO CREATE A GARDEN

LUCY HUNTINGTON

CASSELL&CO

First published in the United Kingdom in 2000 by CASSELL & CO

Design and text copyright © The Ivy Press Limited 2000

A CIP Catalogue record for this book
is available from the British Library

ISBN 0 304 35942 4

This book was conceived,
designed and produced by
THE IVY PRESS LIMITED
The Old Candlemakers, West Street,
Lewes, East Sussex BN7 2NZ

Creative Director: PETER BRIDGEWATER
Designer: SIÂN KEOGH
Editorial Director: DENNY HEMMING
Managing Editor: ANNE TOWNLEY
Illustrations: VANESSA LUFF & PETER BULL
Picture Researcher: LIZ EDDISON

Originated and printed by
Hong Kong Graphic, Hong Kong

This book is typeset in Linotype Perpetua and Univers

CASSELL & CO
Wellington House, 125 Strand, London WC2R 0BB

CONTENTS

INTRODUCTION

Families need gardens: they need an outside space in which to relax, play, dream dreams and grow plants. Most of us have a garden, however microscopic, and many of us have families, but rarely are the two things considered together. Gardens tend to be seen as places in which knowledgeable experts grow specialist plants, not as places where everybody – whatever their age, skills and interests – can have fun exploring and learning to grow a whole range of wonderful plants.

Gardening is not difficult but is a skill readily acquired by anyone, whatever their age and background, and once acquired it can lead to a lifetime of pleasure. Nor does looking after the garden have to be a chore: the key is to keep the garden simple and to discover which plants the various family members enjoy looking after. If nobody likes roses then exclude them from the garden; if someone enjoys growing vegetables then have a vegetable garden; if a teenager turns out to be an alpine enthusiast then give him or her a rock garden. Small children should be encouraged to sow seeds even if they insist on digging them up every day to see how they have grown! There are no right or wrong types of garden or plants, only the wrong choices made by gardeners.

This book is about both planning and planting your family garden: at its core is a directory of the best plants for growing in a family garden, and it also contains lots of exciting ideas for using the featured plants to create an

Gardens used to be thought of as places in which flowers, fruit and vegetables were grown and in which children were expected to play quietly on a restricted range of outdoor equipment. Now all members of the family should be allowed maximum enjoyment and participation in their shared outside space. This may need careful planning and considerable compromise and understanding from everyone.

outside space which is interesting and fun for everyone. Large gardens offer the opportunity to give a separate area to each member of the family, but they can be hard work because they need a lot of maintenance. Small gardens are easier to look after, but need more careful planning to make good use of the space.

The book is divided into three parts. The first explains how to plan your family garden. It starts by showing you how to decide on the most appropriate garden, which will depend on the number of family members, their ages, their particular interests, and the space available. It shows you how to work out what each member of the family wants to be included in the garden and then how to create a garden which is just right for your family – and even how to make sure the family pets can enjoy the garden.

The second part of the book will help you to make informed decisions in selecting materials, features and plants for your garden. There is practical advice on choosing and growing plants and there are details of water features and play equipment.

LEFT *A built-in barbecue on the terrace with an attractive herb garden close by offers a pretty setting for family occasions and for entertaining friends in the open air.*

PLANT DIRECTORY

The final section of this book is the plant directory, which gives details of the most popular and attractive plants for growing in a family garden. Emphasis is placed on tough plants which are easy to grow, as the plants may have to cope with being trampled by dogs, nibbled by pet rabbits or being thumped by the odd football. There may also be limited time available for gardening and the adults concerned may be very new to the task, so the plants need to be capable of thriving even if totally neglected. But even the toughest plants can be beautiful and there are plenty of colourful flowers to ensure your garden looks attractive throughout the year.

Safety is a major consideration where there are small children involved. With this in mind, we have devoted part of the plant directory to plants you may wish to exclude

ABOVE *A family garden needs to have enough variety and interest to please all the generations that use it.*

from your garden, including plants which cause skin allergies, poisonous plants, and plants with prickles and thorns. It is important that these plants can be easily recognized and then removed if necessary.

AN OUTSIDE ROOM

Planning this outside room has not been given enough attention by garden writers. You can seldom find the information you particularly need to help you to understand and guide the gardening interests of each member of the family. This book sets out to encourage families to get outside and use their garden.

Family gardens should be safe, secure havens in which every member of the family, whatever their age, can grow plants and enjoy gardening as well as relax, play, explore and entertain. In this book you will find all you need to ensure that the possibility becomes a reality.

HOW TO USE THIS BOOK

*C*assell's Garden Directories have been conceived and written to appeal both to gardening beginners and to confident gardeners who need advice for a specific project. Each book focuses on a particular type of garden, drawing on the experience of an established expert. The emphasis is on a practical and down-to-earth approach that takes account of the space, time and money that you have available. The ideas and techniques in these books will help you to produce an attractive and manageable garden that you will enjoy for years to come.

Cassell's Directory of Plants for Family Gardens looks at ways to make use of garden space to create an outside room that offers something to all the members of your family. The book is divided into three sections. The opening section, *Planning Your Garden*, considers the requirements of different age groups and looks at some of the issues you will need to address. There are also three inspirational garden plans for making the most of a surburban garden, a small country garden, and a very small town garden.

Part Two of the book, *Creating Your Garden*, moves on to the nitty-gritty of putting your ideas into practice. This section opens with some advice on the range of different features that you can choose from, such as furniture, hard surfaces, play equipment, and fountains and ponds. There is also advice on producing a lawn that will be appropriate for the range of demands that your family is going to put on it; also on the selection, buying and planting of appropriate shrubs, herbs and flowers.

The remainder of Part Two is packed with practical information on basic techniques such as sowing and feeding plants, repairing damaged lawns, making compost and supporting climbers. Moving on from this basic grounding, this section then encourages you to put your skills to work with a series of specific projects such as making wildlife areas and creating a children's garden. There are step-by-step illustrations throughout this section that show clearly and simply what you need to do to achieve the best results. Also included are handy hints and tips, points to watch out for, and star plants that are particularly suitable for the projects that are described.

The final part of the book, *The Plant Directory*, is a comprehensive listing of all the plants mentioned in the earlier sections, together with other plants that are suitable for a family garden. Each plant is illustrated, and symbols add information on appropriate growing conditions, speed of growth and ease of maintenance.

GARDEN SCHEMES are included to inspire you to great things in your own garden.

COLOUR PHOTOGRAPHS show what can be achieved with a little effort and imagination.

3D PLANS show the best planting scheme for you to achieve the ideal outcome.

THE KEY FEATURES of the plan are described to help you visualize the final effect.

CHOICES SPREADS show a selection of plants, garden furniture or other features that might be appropriate in your garden.

COLOUR PHOTOGRAPHS help you to decide on the appropriate feature for your garden.

EXPLANATORY TEXT describes the various possibilities available in each category.

THE CHECKLIST details important things to look out for in choosing garden features.

CLEAR ILLUSTRATIONS show each step of the process.

PRACTICAL SPREADS give useful information on basic techniques and garden projects.

WATCHPOINTS BOXES give a checklist of cautions and problems to look out for.

CLEAR DESCRIPTIVE TEXT details the appearance and the appropriate growing conditions for each plant.

THE PLANT DIRECTORY is organized into categories, making it simple to find a particular type of plant.

THE SYMBOLS PANEL gives important information on features such as speed of growth and shade-tolerance.

COLOUR PHOTOGRAPHS clearly identify each plant listed.

SIDEBAR shows at a glance the season of interest for each plant.

1

PLANNING YOUR GARDEN

Before starting to design your ideal family garden, you need to consider the various requirements of all the family members, including the pets. Finding space for a terrace for meals, a barbecue, a sandpit and paddling pool, a tree-house and climbing frame, some areas for privacy and peace, not to mention beds and borders for the gardening members of the family may sound like a tall order. However, with careful planning you should be able to satisfy at least some of each person's wishes.

LEFT *Even a tiny garden can have a patch of lawn for children to run, jump and play on.*

WHAT IS A FAMILY GARDEN?

A family garden is any outside space that is expected to fulfil the needs of a range of family members. Most people at some time in their lives will have a garden, and this may or may not coincide with having a family, but only a minority of the population are knowledgeable about gardening.

A family can be as small as a single parent and child, can be the conventional mother, father and two children, or it can extend to include grandparents, parents, whether biological or otherwise, and any number of children, step-children, aunts, uncles and partners. In this book, a family has been taken to mean all the people, related or not, who share the same outside space, and will usually include one or more children.

Families also include all ages, from the new baby to toddlers, school children, teenagers, young adults, and right through to middle-aged and elderly relatives. The needs of an 80-year-old great granny are going to be very different to those of a newborn baby, a rebellious teenager or young parents. Family gardens are often taken to imply families with children, but in this book we have tried to look at the needs of all age groups.

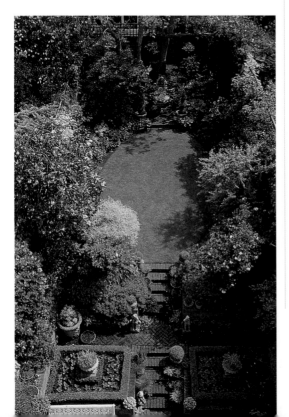

LEFT *This narrow garden has been built on three levels to make good use of the limited space. Parents can relax on the terrace while the children play on the lawn below.*

THEN AND NOW

A family garden used to be a place in which vegetables were grown to feed the family; there was plenty of space to hang out the washing; and there was a patch of lawn on which the baby's pram was put out in the afternoon. Now the family garden can be any garden, whatever its size and location, in which all the various members of the family can indulge in gardening or any other outdoor activity.

CHILDREN OF ALL AGES

Babies are easy to accommodate in the garden as they just need a flat, smooth surface in the shade on which they can lie and play. Once they can crawl and start walking, however, the garden becomes an exciting place to explore. At this stage, safety becomes a major consideration, and plenty of playing space should be provided within sight of the house. More details and ideas for small children in the garden are on pages 18 and 19.

Gardens are great places for school-age children, especially if they can have their own space where they can dig, play and even garden without annoying other members of the family – see pages 20 and 21 for further ideas.

If your family includes teenagers, then you already know that, if they use the garden, it is for talking to friends, playing music, sleeping and eating. They value their privacy and want their own private space. In a larger garden it may be possible to offer them their own area at the far end. Ideally this should be screened and include an area for sitting and lounging or, if possible, a couple of trees with a hammock and even a large swing. Add a locked shed in which they can keep their special bits and pieces, and they should be happy.

PARENTS NEED GARDENS

Parents are often forgotten when planning gardens. Every effort is made to accommodate sandpits, swings and rabbit hutches for the children, and the fact that there are adult members of the family can appear unimportant. However, once issues of safety are resolved, then there should be room for comfortable chairs on the terrace for relaxing and the inclusion of the borders and garden features that the adults will enjoy.

KEEPING GRANDPARENTS HAPPY

Today an extended family may well include a grandparent who may or may not be elderly, and there may be visiting members of the family who are less active than they used to be. The family garden needs to cater for their needs, which may include somewhere to sit out in the sun or the shade, interesting things to look at, and perhaps their own area of garden. People who have retired from work are often keen gardeners, in which case the plants and garden features that are chosen will need to be those that they enjoy looking after.

FAMILY PETS

These all-important four-legged family members should not be forgotten in planning your garden: see pages 22 and 23 for details of how to cater for their various needs and requirements.

LEFT *The end of this garden has been laid out with a summer-house and a sandpit.*

WHAT DO YOU NEED IN YOUR FAMILY GARDEN?

*M*ost gardens are modest in size, and it is almost inevitable that the limited room available will necessitate some careful planning. It is always worth preparing a checklist of activities, features and plants that you want to include. You will, of course, have to prioritize your needs and desires, working together as a family to decide on joint goals. Try to see the limits imposed on you by your garden – whether of size, shape or location – not as problems but as challenges.

When only one member of the family has charge of the garden and dictates how it is to be planted and developed, then there is only one person whose wishes need to be satisfied. For a whole family, however, there probably needs to be a more democratic process at work. Even when members of the family are too young to put their gardening preferences into words, their particular requirements should also be taken into account *(see pages 18 and 19)*.

There are various different ways of looking at how you might plan the garden, and you might start by considering the type of garden that you all want. It might include some or all of the following features, depending on the resources at your disposal:

BELOW *A bird feeder is a perennial favourite in the family garden.*

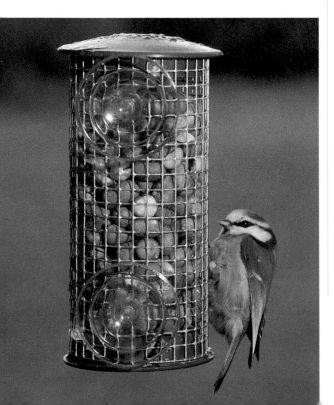

❖ An outdoor living space for eating, reading and relaxing.
❖ A place for entertaining friends and family and for parties.
❖ An adventure playground for children, with slides, swings, rope ladders, tree-houses and a climbing frame.
❖ A gardener's garden full of roses, herbaceous borders, trees, hedges, spring bulbs and shrubs for autumn colour.
❖ A productive garden full of vegetables and fruit.
❖ A wildlife garden with birds, bees and butterflies.
❖ A tranquil oasis of peace, quiet and gentle fountains.
❖ A place for recreation and exercise – complete with football pitch, swimming pool and tennis court.
❖ A pets' corner for dogs, cats, rabbits and guinea pigs.

MAKING LISTS

One way of sorting out what is wanted is to sit everyone down and ask them to make a list of what they would like in a garden. Babies' considerations will have to be taken

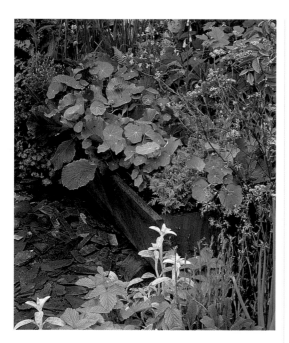

ABOVE *A special corner brought to life with a child's 'trough garden' filled with nasturtiums and French marigolds.*

POINTS TO CONSIDER

MOTHER AND FATHER
- ☐ Terrace for family meals
- ☐ Barbecue
- ☐ Safety
- ☐ Water
- ☐ Time to enjoy
- ☐ Somewhere to read
- ☐ Rose arch/beds
- ☐ Scent
- ☐ Camellias
- ☐ Easy maintenance

GRANDPARENTS
- ☐ Comfortable chair
- ☐ Roses
- ☐ Herb garden
- ☐ Place to watch grandchildren playing
- ☐ Bird table
- ☐ Water feature

16-YEAR-OLD GIRL
- ☐ My own space
- ☐ Hammock
- ☐ Swimming pool
- ☐ No kids
- ☐ No gardening
- ☐ Music

5-YEAR-OLD GIRL
- ☐ Pink flowers
- ☐ Pretty flowers
- ☐ My own garden
- ☐ Playhouse
- ☐ Swing
- ☐ Picnic place

UNCLE
- ☐ Vegetable garden
- ☐ Shed
- ☐ Greenhouse
- ☐ Peace and quiet
- ☐ Barbecue

10-YEAR-OLD BOY
- ☐ Frogs and insects
- ☐ Adventure playground
- ☐ Campsite
- ☐ Barbecue
- ☐ A private den
- ☐ Football pitch

3-YEAR-OLD BOY
- ☐ Paddling pool
- ☐ Sandpit
- ☐ Tadpoles
- ☐ Slide and swings
- ☐ Fish

into account by the adults, but allow any children who are old enough to offer their own ideas. It may help in the list-making if memory joggers are used, for instance suggesting that everybody puts down their favourite flowers. It is useful if family members prioritize their chosen features, stating which are the most important.

An alternative is for one member of the family to make a list of everything that could be included in a garden and then to circulate the list for each family member to tick the items of importance to them.

Lists can include features (a paddling pool, a wildlife pond); feelings (peace, relaxation, excitement); use of space (place to entertain friends, to read, to have adventures); or types of plants (roses, pink flowers, scent, apple trees).

MAKING CHOICES

When the lists are complete, you can see if any of the items on different lists are compatible and which wishes are totally impossible. Looking at the sample lists above, several family members want a barbecue, so that needs to be considered; a swimming pool is probably just a dream given the cost, space and safety aspects, but the football player might be satisfied with goalposts if he cannot have a whole football pitch. Everybody wants their own space, so plan for some secluded sitting areas, and a rose garden with a rose arch would keep several people happy. Room needs to be found for a sandpit and a paddling pool, if possible, and somewhere for frogs. By considering everybody's wishes, a compromise can be reached.

AN OUTSIDE ROOM

*T*he garden should be seen as another room in which all the activities that take place inside the house – eating, sleeping, relaxing, playing, entertaining and even cooking – can occur. A paved terrace adjacent to the house usually provides the space for this outside room.

Measure how much room is taken up if all the family members sit together around a table, remembering that you need space to push a chair away from the table to get up. A lawn adjacent to the terrace allows family and guests to spread out into the garden, but when the lawn is wet everybody will want to stay on the terrace. A paved area of 3.6 x 4.5m (12 x 15ft) allows eight people to sit comfortably around a table; extend this to 4 x 5.4m (13 x 18ft) and there is room to stand for drinks beforehand.

POSITION OF THE TERRACE

If you want breakfast in the sun, the terrace needs to be on the east side of the house; for a sunny lunch, place the terrace to the south; and for the warmth of the setting sun for an evening meal or barbecue, then a west-facing terrace is perfect. A terrace facing southwest is ideal, allowing some shade if the sun is too hot and providing a warm spot for afternoon siestas and evening parties.

When orienting the terrace, take account of the position of any outside doors or French windows that give easy access to the house. If the only access is a door around the corner from the terrace, plan a wide path between them.

EATING IN THE GARDEN

Most families will want to eat, at least occasionally, in the garden, and some may even want to dine out every time the weather is remotely warm and dry enough. Main meals

ABOVE *A very stylish modern terrace with wooden decking to match the indoor flooring.*

are best served at a table on the terrace, which will be close to the house for serving and clearing up. Other meals may be more fun as picnics carried into the garden.

Barbecues can be built into the terrace, or they can be free-standing. Some have wheels so that they can be moved away after use. There are various sizes, but if you are new to barbecue cookery, get a small portable one first so that you can find the best spot for it – out of the wind, near the kitchen and accessible to both cook and guests – and also to see if you think barbecuing is for you. If you decide to proceed, buy a larger and more robust portable barbecue, or, if you are really keen, build your own.

POINTS TO CONSIDER

🍃 Decisions on a barbecue should be made by the whole family, as non-cooking members are often quite happy to take over the job of barbecuing from the regular cook.

🍃 Use garden flares and candles with caution, always placing them out of any wind and where there is no danger of fire should they fall over.

🐾 It used to be the case that terraces were too small for practical use, or often included beds and borders of low plants within the paving. Nowadays the paved area is more often an extension of the house, and so it needs to be planned for maximum use by the whole family.

FAMILY GATHERINGS

Gardens are wonderful places for family gatherings and parties, allowing for a convivial atmosphere and offering plenty of room for mingling, while providing secluded corners for more intimate moments. You can create extra seating by including some raised beds or low walls to the side of the terrace; the walls should have wide copings at sitting height (45cm/18in for adults and 30–40cm/12–16in for children) on which you can place cushions when seats are needed. Raised beds allow plants to be placed safely out of the way of children playing on the terrace, and low walls give a greater feeling of privacy.

For children's birthday parties the garden is an ideal setting, providing the weather is dry and not too windy. Any mess can be easily cleared up and there is plenty of room for organized games to get rid of youthful energy. Tea can be served around the table or perhaps as a special picnic, always a popular treat.

LIGHTING

If you do lots of entertaining, or the family likes to use the garden in the evening, then you might consider lighting the terrace or perhaps the whole of the garden. Candles and lamps are convenient for occasional use but a full-scale electric lighting scheme can transform an ordinary family garden into a place of magic and mystery. There are many light fittings from which to choose, but always use lights and cabling that are designed for outside use. You should obtain the advice of a qualified electrician before beginning any kind of electrical installation.

BELOW *A cottage garden with dinner set for two – a welcome treat after the children have gone to bed and the buckets and spades and tricycles have been cleared away.*

UNDER-FIVES IN THE GARDEN

If you have young children, your garden should be designed to provide a safe outside space for them to explore. During the first two years, a child progresses from a helpless, totally dependent being, to a speaking, running person with a mind and a will of its own. The baby safely ensconced with a few toys on a rug very quickly becomes an active toddler trying to climb trees or escape over the garden gate.

Traditionally, the garden was the place in which babies were placed to sleep in their prams in the afternoon, protected by a net against marauding cats, and with a sunshade to screen them from direct sunlight. This established part of the daily routine ended with the demise of the large pram in favour of more portable buggies. Now babies are more likely to sleep in the house and spend their waking hours in the garden.

Much of a baby's time can be spent in the garden, as long as there is a suitable surface and the weather is fine. A padded mat on the paving or a rug on the grass provide a comfortable base for most activities, but do remember that small babies should always be in the shade, even if the sun is not actually shining. The drawback to outside playing is that babies must not be left alone, particularly when they begin to crawl; when awake, they will demand the full attention of at least one member of the family, and will need a range of toys to keep them happily occupied.

TODDLERS AND THE UNDER-THREES

Once children can walk they are able to get everywhere, but because they are incapable of understanding the meaning of danger, safety becomes a top priority *(see pages 48 and 49)*. They need a flat part of the garden allocated to their play needs that can be used all year, preferably with some grass for use in summer and a paved area for year-round play. For their safety, the area needs to be in full view of the windows of the house at all times. There should also be a shady space for when the sun gets too hot, as small children are very susceptible to heatstroke.

The most sensible areas are the terrace and that part of the lawn nearest the house. The only problems are that the space may be taken up by garden furniture which can create interesting but potentially dangerous obstacles for small children, and that their brightly coloured toys are

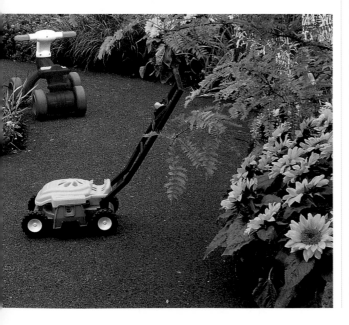

WATCHPOINTS

🍃 If you have very young children, take particular care on where you choose to site a pool. Children should be in view at all times, as a young infant can drown in just a few centimetres of water.

🍃 Make sure all boundaries are secure and child-proof.

🍃 Avoid rough surfaces such as gravel for play areas.

LEFT *This blue rubberized path makes an ideal surface for toddlers and wheeled toys,* *although most people will probably not want to customize their garden to this extent.*

POINTS TO CONSIDER

�ـ Determine where a child's interest lies and encourage it –
if they want to water the garden, get them a watering can.
�ـ Be prepared for a mess – mud pies can be fun!
�ـ Sandpits are not just for toddlers – older children also
enjoy excavation, though on a larger scale.

an eyesore for other members of the family. The answer is
to bring the toys inside after use and to have easily movable
garden furniture if the terrace space is restricted.

SANDPITS

From the earliest age children love digging and filling. You
can construct a simple sandpit by digging a hole in the
lawn, lining the sides of the hole with wooden boards and
the base with 10cm (4in) of hardcore or coarse gravel
covered with a geo-textile membrane, and then filling the
hole with sand. An alternative is to dig a hole in the terrace,
put blocks at the sides to support the paving, and line and
fill as before. The third option, and usually the most
popular, is to buy a preformed plastic sandpit that can sit
on the lawn or terrace. The problems here are that these
sandpits are fairly small, and the bright colour of the plastic
is visually intrusive. Choose a sandpit with a well-fitting
lid to prevent cats using it and to keep the sand dry.

Paddling pools nearly always accompany sandpits, the
two recreating the seaside experience in the garden. A
small collapsible pool is most sensible for the early years,
as it can be put away easily after use.

GARDENING WITH SMALL CHILDREN

Once children are toddling, they will want to be involved
with whatever is going on, especially if it looks messy, so
if you try to garden they will want to garden with you.
Buy a set of children's gardening tools, including a wheel-
barrow, trowel, fork, rake, spade and watering can, and
allow them to work with you. It may take longer to get
the work done, but everybody should have fun, and you
will be preparing the ground for their green-fingered
future. Watering seems to hold a fascination for this age

group, so allow children to
help; it may not be very
effective but they will enjoy
themselves.

ABOVE *A small sandpit can
be tucked into a corner of the
garden. Add a hosepipe and
you have the seaside at home!*

Do remember that fun activities in the garden do not
necessarily involve sophisticated and expensive toys. Slides
and swings are nice if you have them, but the old tried-
and-tested favourites such as balls, bouncers, buckets and
spades, and blocks are still the best.

TRIKES, BIKES AND TOY CARS

All children like whizzing around on wheels, so you may
need to accommodate tricycles, bikes, toy cars and
scooters. The garden is a much safer space in which to learn
to master new skills than the public road or the park, and
an area of dry, close-mown grass is ideal. As riders become
more adventurous, they need a smooth, hard riding
surface: asphalt or concrete is best but neither is very
attractive. An area of well-laid paving within sight of the
house windows is perfect for the tricycle riders, but a
negotiable path around the garden is greater fun for more
adventurous cyclists.

SCHOOL-AGE CHILDREN

Once children have reached school age, they can be given the freedom of the garden. This is an age when space is needed to kick footballs, build camps, dig holes and perhaps have their own garden. The garden needs to be a place for adventure and exploration, with hidden secret places and wildlife corners. The only problem is keeping boisterous ten-year-olds away from other members of the family who want peace and quiet.

The answer is to separate some of the activities for this age group into their own space, where physically possible. Within this area they should be free to play games, dig holes, and entertain their friends, but they must understand that other parts of the garden are to be shared and that some areas are off limits or at least to be treated with respect. The same delineation should be made in the garden as is found in the house, with children's bedrooms and playrooms being their areas, the family sitting room being shared, and the parents' bedroom off limits. This idea works well when the garden is large enough for several separate spaces, but may be difficult to achieve in smaller gardens. Where space is restricted, family members will simply have to learn to accommodate one another's needs.

ACTIVITIES

Children in this age group vary enormously in the activities they enjoy. Some will like studying insects and plants and reading quietly; others want to do nothing but kick footballs and play rowdy games; yet others will play long games of make-believe in the undergrowth. Wait until children express a wish, or show an interest, before installing play equipment or garden toys: there is no point setting up goalposts if nobody is interested in football.

ADVENTURE

Most children of this age love adventures, and a garden designed with hidden paths, secret shrub areas and a few large rocks can become the setting for elaborate games of make-believe. The larger the area the better, but it should not be so large that children can become lost or frightened.

WATCHPOINTS

🍂 Always ensure that children feel safe in their garden. If they find an area frightening, such as a shadowy shrubbery, try to find a way of making it seem friendlier.
🍂 When children start on excavations, always keep a check on the position and depth of holes, and keep younger children away.

LEFT *A fun container garden which would be a certain winner as the children's entry in the local flower show (make sure the owner doesn't need the boots any more).*

Almost all children love playing games, whether on their own, in a twosome, or with a crowd of friends and family. There are lots of games that can be played in the garden, not all of which need a lawn or lots of room.

- A basketball net fixed to a house or garage wall can give hours of pleasure to keen basketball players.
- Laying paving slabs on the terrace or a side path that can be marked and used for hopscotch is very easy.
- An enlarged sandpit can be used for a game of boule when the bucket-and-spade brigade are in bed or occupied elsewhere.
- A table tennis table can be set up on any flat area of concrete, asphalt or smooth paving.

CAMPSITES

Camping can involve simply putting up a tepee for an afternoon. At the other extreme, you could set up a tent for the summer and offer the chance to sleep out in the garden, with meals around a campfire. If a tent is to be erected for more than one day, it should be sited where it doesn't matter if the underlying grass gets damaged. Tents with integral groundsheets can be sited on sand, bark or bare soil.

DIGGING HOLES

Some children love digging holes, and the deeper the better. This requires a spare area, and light, easily dug topsoil and subsoil. It could be a part of the vegetable garden between crops, as long as all holes are filled in once the ground is needed for cropping.

GAMES ON GRASS

Even a small lawn can be used for game playing. Swingball needs a relatively small circle, as do swing football and clock golf. A crazy golf course can be set up in whatever space is available, including along grass paths and any side lawns. A soccer goal merely needs space in front to aim the ball and some tough plants that can survive being hit.

Larger, more regularly shaped areas are needed for French cricket and rounders, depending on the age and ability of the players. Short tennis and badminton need a 13.5 x 6m (44 x 20ft) rectangular area for the court, but will also need additional grass around the court for players to serve and run out. Wherever games are to be played, the lawn area needs to be surrounded by tough plants that are hardy enough to survive children rushing in among them to retrieve balls, and being hit by balls and the rackets and sticks of frustrated players.

BELOW *A children's lookout – an excellent alternative to a tree-house where there is no suitable tree available.*

FAMILY PETS

Your garden may also need to accommodate the family pets. Whatever the number and types of animals concerned, they need to be carefully considered when planning your garden. Lack of good planning can lead to disaster: the cat might use the sandpit as a litter tray, the rabbits might escape from their hutch and eat all your lettuces, and the dog might create brown circles on the lawn. With a little foresight, your garden can become a comfortable home for all your family pets.

Dogs can be great companions for all members of the family, but their needs will have to be accommodated within the garden. Make sure that the garden is escape-proof, with secure surrounding fences or walls and gates. This containment can be dual purpose and keep small children safe as well. If you have a new puppy, make sure that the fence and gates will still be high enough to prevent escape when the dog is fully grown.

Bored dogs can become destructive and may start digging craters in a favourite rose bed or in a dearly loved children's garden, so there should be room for the dog to play and exercise, and areas to sit in both sun and shade. An outside kennel will give it a sheltered and shady place that is its own special territory within the garden.

No matter how often a dog is exercised, all dogs will on occasion use the garden as a toilet. Faeces should be removed as soon as possible, and disposed of either in the household waste or in a dog-loo sunk into a spare area of the garden. Unfortunately, bitches' urine tends to burn holes in the lawn, so they need to be trained to use a corner of the garden. Male dogs urinating on edible plants can create a health hazard; if the dog cannot be kept away from these areas, then you should fence off the vegetable garden or grow herbs and salad plants in raised beds.

Some dogs love water: labradors will jump into any pond, however small, and can cause havoc with the carefully nurtured life in your wildlife pond. In a small garden it is probably a case of training the dog to keep out of the water, or installing a wall or pebble fountain instead.

CATS

Unlike dogs, cats are independent animals, living their own lives most of the time and condescending to join in our lives when they feel like it. Like dogs, they can get bored, and enjoy sharpening their claws, so give them their own personal scratching post rather than leaving them to remove the bark of a newly planted tree.

Cats will find their own exercise, but many of them love climbing, and children's tree-houses might have been custom-made for cats. They spend much of their time sleeping, and prefer a warm area of paving in the sun, preferably where they won't be trodden on by small feet.

They are clean animals and like to dig holes for their toilet arrangements, and cover them after use. This may not matter in the established parts of the garden but it is a real nuisance if they choose the children's sandpit. The

LEFT *This attractive and unusual rabbit hutch can be moved around the garden to avoid damage to the grass. Children will also enjoy looking after chickens: they are relatively easy to care for and home-laid eggs are always a treat.*

🐾 A possibility for a larger garden would be a dovecote with resident white doves.

🐾 If you want free-range eggs, give your chickens the run of the garden during daytime, but be prepared to hunt for the eggs in the undergrowth.

🐾 It is impossible to keep cats in a garden unless you build a high wall around the whole boundary.

answer is to have a cover for the sandpit and to give the cat its own sand toilet elsewhere in the garden.

ABOVE *The family cat may be inclined to attack birds, so do fit a small bell on a cat collar to warn birds of the danger.*

As a special treat for your family cat, plant some plants for it to enjoy like catmint *(see page 78)*. This is a real favourite with cats and they will eat it, roll on it, and finally sleep in it. Plant a couple of plants to allow for damage, and you might find it necessary initially to fence off the plants to get them successfully established.

Cats and birds are not really compatible, so you may have to choose between attracting birds and accommodating the family cat. One proven method of keeping the two apart is to put a bell on a the cat's collar to warn birds when it is on the prowl.

HAZARDS

🐾 Geese can become territorial and aggressive and may decide to keep everyone else out of the garden!

🐾 A guinea pig or rabbit run should have a wire mesh floor to prevent the animals from digging out and escaping.

🐾 Animal faeces can be a health hazard, so make sure that animals do not foul play areas.

🐾 Family pets, especially dogs, can be jealous of a new baby, so keep a watch on your pet for the first few weeks to make sure that all is well.

RABBITS AND GUINEA PIGS

Rabbits and guinea pigs are easy to tame and like being handled by children; they are social animals and prefer to be kept in pairs. To avoid excessive breeding, ensure that you keep two females together, or keep a rabbit with a guinea pig, as they seem to enjoy sharing accommodation.

Both animals need housing that can stay outside in the summer, plus the protection of a shed or outbuilding in the winter. The hutch needs two compartments, one for sleeping and the other for feeding, and should be raised off the ground for ventilation. Place it where it is easily accessible and enjoys sun for at least part of the day. Both animals enjoy exercise and need a safe area in which to run. A portable run that can be moved around the lawn is better then a permanent enclosure.

TORTOISES

Tortoises are just great fun to watch as they slowly trundle over the garden or munch a lettuce leaf. They can be given the whole garden as their territory or be restricted to one area. A special tortoise house will provide shade from the sun and can be used for winter hibernation.

BIRDS

Chickens, ducks and geese can all be kept as pets. Chickens, particularly bantams, make good pets for slightly older children, who will enjoy looking after them and collecting the eggs. They need hen coops to roost in at night for protection from foxes, and enclosed runs that can be moved around the garden.

In a larger garden, there may be room to include a few ducks, preferably with their own duckpond, and even a few geese. The latter make excellent watch animals.

PREPARING A PLAN – A SURVEY

To get the most out of your garden it is essential to plan the overall layout before making decisions on the details: that is, you should plan where the rose beds are to go before deciding which roses to plant. Again, all members of the family can be involved in the planning process, from surveying the garden to working out the plan on paper. An involvement at this early stage should make everyone feel that this is their garden.

To create a well-designed garden you need to compose a series of linked 'pictures', each with one of your chosen garden features at the centre. Place each feature carefully so that it forms the centre of the picture: a seat lined up with the path, a sundial in the exact centre of a herb garden, a path leading to the trunk of an existing tree. You may want to improve your garden 'pictures' by enhancing your features: the sundial may look better on a circle of paving; the seat might have a hedge behind it, or an arch over it; the tree trunk may need a seat or a patch of white flowers at its base.

SURVEYING YOUR GARDEN

The first step is to draw a plan of your garden. This may sound impossibly difficult but in reality it is quite easy. You may already have an architect's plan that includes the garden; if so, you can copy it onto a fresh piece of paper. If no plan exists, then proceed through the following steps:

1. Draw a rough sketch of the house and garden on a piece of paper. Label each corner of the site and the corners of the house with a letter. If you have both a front and back garden, it is usually easier to make two plans.
2. Next you need to measure the garden accurately. Use a long measuring tape or metre rule and measure the length of each boundary of the garden, i.e. along a straight line between the points you have labelled on your plan.
3. Having measured all the boundaries, measure across the plot between opposite corners. These cross measurements are vital to be sure that you get the shape of the garden accurately recorded on your plan.
4. You will also need to measure the walls of the house that are adjacent to the garden. Start at a corner and check the positions of any windows and doors as you proceed. If there is a gap between the house and boundary, be sure to measure this accurately.
5. Existing garden features that you want to keep, for example established trees, need to be measured from one of the boundaries. Find the distance up the line and then, at right angles to the boundary line, measure the distance to the feature. Check the size of the tree trunk and the spread of the tree's branches, as these may affect how you use or plant the area next to the tree.

SITE ANALYSIS

While you are surveying, check other factors that may affect how you plan the area. Use a compass to find the position of north, which will indicate which areas of the garden are sunny and which are shady. If cold winds are a problem, note any sheltered parts of the garden. You also need to look out of the garden to establish any good views that are to be kept and any ugly views that may need to be screened.

LEFT *You will probably be happy to keep some of the existing features in your garden survey.*

DRAWING UP THE PLAN

You now need to select a scale. The easiest method is to use the centimetres marked on your ruler, using either 1cm to represent 1m on the ground – a scale of 1:100 – or 2cm for every 1m – a scale of 1:50. Start by drawing the longest boundary line to scale on a piece of graph paper, and mark the ends AB as on your sketch. To find the next point, C, stretch a geometry compass along your ruler to the scale length of line AC, place the compass point on A and draw an arc for C. Repeat the same process for line BC; where the compass arcs cross is point C.

Repeat this process for the other corners, and then plot the position of the house including the doors and windows. Finally, plot the existing features using your ruler to find the distance up the boundary line, and then the distance into the feature.

FUNCTIONAL PLAN

Once you have a scale drawing of your garden, you can start allocating areas for the various items on the family lists. Start with the terrace area near the house, making sure it is large enough, and then the lawn. Find a sunny spot for vegetables and for sitting areas. Allocate space for any children's dens or tree-houses, and any private areas for teenagers. Decide on sizes and positions of flower beds. Check that the area where younger children will play with their toys is safe and in view of the house, and that they have somewhere to try out their first set of wheels. If a pond is on the list, then consider where it might be placed. Finally, take into account the various needs of your pets.

WATCHPOINTS

🍂 Be sure to read and write down measurements carefully – 6 and 9, and 4 and 7, are easily confused.

🍂 Select either feet or metres for your measurements, choosing whichever system you prefer. Using unfamiliar units may lead to problems.

🍂 Have one person in charge – too many surveyors will definitely spoil the plan.

🍂 Avoid wet and windy days – a tape measure blowing in the wind is impossible to use accurately, and it is very difficult to record details on wet paper.

ABOVE *A new house where there has never been a garden gives you the ideal opportunity to create a space that suits your family without having to undo other people's mistakes.*

To complete the plan, you need to consider how to link the various areas of the garden. Will access be across the lawn or will you need to put in some paths? If you are going to have paths, you need to decide whether you want them to be paved or grass, and whether the shape should be curved or straight.

A SUBURBAN GARDEN

Where the garden is of a reasonable size it may be possible to have separate features or areas for the different age groups in the family. The first thing to consider is the position and size of the terrace and then the shape of the lawn. Once these have been established, you can then start fitting in all the other features required.

This garden is a typical rectangular shape and lies to the southeast at the back of the house. It is relatively flat and surrounded by a 1.8m (6ft) high closeboard fence. In planning the garden it was decided to use circular shapes for most of the features in order to soften the strong, straight lines of the fence, and to allow for a curving path around the garden. The three existing trees were attractive, so the plan had to allow for their retention and continued growth.

It is important to have good views into the garden from the windows of the house; the pebble fountain has been placed directly in front of the kitchen window and the herb garden is clearly seen from the sitting room. The terrace leads directly onto the lawn to allow the younger children to play on both surfaces, and there is a sandpit readily

POINTS TO CONSIDER

🌢 Be careful to allow for the continuing growth of existing trees – check their ultimate height and spread in a reliable reference book.

🌢 Use simple shapes for features like the herb garden and then repeat the shape elsewhere in the garden.

🌢 Use paving materials which reflect the materials, or the colour of the materials, used in building the house.

visible from the sitting room or the terrace. The sandpit can be turned into a planted area when no longer needed.

A path encircles the lawn and doubles as a mowing strip and as a track for tricycles, toy cars and other vehicles. The path also leads into and around the herb garden with its central sundial. This could be for culinary herbs for the kitchen, or a collection of coloured-leaved herbs like golden marjoram and purple sage, or a mixture of both. Many herbs attract bees, including winter savory, thyme, lavender and hyssop, so in summer this area will be alive with the buzz of bees collecting nectar.

Part of the area at the far end of the garden is left semi-wild for school-age children to have a place of their own for exploration and adventure. There is room for a wildlife hide, a pond and a clump of berrying shrubs to provide food for birds in autumn and winter. In the corner is an attractive wooden swing, strong enough for most adults as well as children.

Space is left for several seats around the garden so that there are sitting areas in both sun and shade. There are a selection of planted areas, in sun and part shade, so if the parents are keen gardeners they can include many of their favourite plants. There is room for a child's garden and a locked shed for tools and chemicals.

LEFT *A well-made, sturdy swing in a corner of the garden, ready to give pleasure to all members of the family.*

The comfortable arbour has a seat for older members of the family to enjoy peace and quiet and watch the bees at work.

The vegetable garden and compost heap are surrounded by a low fence with a gate. There is a bed along the fence for growing cordon and espalier fruit.

A large central lawn allows a clear view into most of the garden and lots of space for toys and games.

A safe water feature is placed near the house, surrounded by planting to attract butterflies.

The semicircular terrace is large enough for at least eight people to sit down for a meal.

This area will be made into a wildlife pond when the younger children have got past the age when a pond is considered to be a safety hazard.

ABOVE *This is a plan for a medium-sized garden, 20m x 12m (65ft x 39ft), in a town where the family has several children of different ages and a dependent relative. There are three existing trees and the house is to the northwest of the garden.*

A SMALL COUNTRY GARDEN

A small garden requires more careful planning than a large one, especially when the requirements of all the family have to be taken into account. It is possible to create a very attractive and user-friendly garden which all the family can enjoy, although it may be necessary to eliminate some desirable features to achieve a workable solution. A relatively small garden can be sub-divided to create separate 'rooms', each of which can be designed for a specific use. These can be enclosed, with gated access if required.

This design is for an irregularly shaped garden at the end of a row of houses, with neighbours on one side. From the upstairs windows, there are views out over the countryside to the south and east. The garden is accessible through the conservatory, and also through the playroom.

The garden was designed to feature several distinct areas in order to accommodate the different needs of the various members of the family. It was also important to plan a really attractive view from the kitchen window, where the sink is sited.

THREE ROOMS

Three areas have been created, including a paved terrace, enclosed vegetable garden and a lawn surrounded by beds and borders. The terrace area includes a small butterfly garden, also a herb garden, which has a pot of variegated lemon balm as a central feature. The terrace leads into both the other areas, with three steps up to the vegetable garden and a flat grass path to the lawn. The children can sit or play on the steps and the low wall but, while they are still young, a locked gate prevents them from entering the vegetable garden and causing havoc.

There is a bird bath situated in the middle of the vegetable garden, which can be seen both from the kitchen

ABOVE *In a family garden, one of the main considerations is the provision of an area that can host a table and chairs, so that meals can be enjoyed outside.*

and when standing on the terrace. As well as allowing plenty of room for the cultivation of fresh food for the kitchen, the vegetable garden also has a compost bin and a seat so that you can have a well-earned rest after digging the potatoes!

The lawn is clearly visible from the kitchen and the conservatory. Although it is not large enough for a game of football, there is enough space for a paddling pool and the younger children's toys. There is a range of planted areas around the lawn, both in the sun and partly in shade. One bed is planted with berrying plants to attract birds. There is another small border that could be annexed by a child for his or her own garden. A sloping grass path leads up into the vegetable garden through a second gate.

An almost secret path runs the length of the hedge to allow access for hedge cutting and to the concealed cat's lavatory. Finally, tucked behind the corner of the house, there is a shed standing on a paved area for outside storage.

POINTS TO CONSIDER

🍃 Check whether the boundary walls or fences belong to you or your neighbour before embarking on any work.

🍃 Trellis forms a very attractive division in a small garden, taking up very little room and providing a great support for climbing plants.

🍃 Make the paved area as big as you can, so there is plenty of space for children to play and for the family to eat.

The low wall that separates the vegetable garden from the terrace is just the right height to provide extra seating when needed.

An extended terrace outside the playroom and kitchen has space for a table and four chairs, lots of toys, possibly a reclining chair or two, and a sandpit if desired.

A raised vegetable garden surrounded by a trellis planted with cordon fruit trees and blackberries.

There is room on the lawn for children to play; also for an inflatable paddling pool.

At the far side of the lawn a seat has been placed under the existing tree to provide a shady retreat. By adding a folding table, informal meals could be eaten here.

The trellis surrounding the vegetable area has lockable gates to keep children and animals out.

ABOVE This is a plan for an irregularly shaped garden approximately 17m x 10m (56ft x 33ft). The house is the last on the street, and is separated from the adjoining field by a hedge. The family has three small children and a cat.

A VERY SMALL TOWN GARDEN

Small gardens in the middle of towns are often shaded by surrounding walls and houses, making it difficult for grass to grow really well. In such cases, it often makes better sense to pave the whole garden, leaving interesting spaces for planting. The garden can then be planned as a single outside room that includes as many functions and features as are feasible. The walls can be decorated with shade-loving climbers — flowering varieties to add colour and evergreen species to enhance privacy.

This is a plan for a city garden, which originally consisted of a few concrete slabs and a scruffy lawn sloping up to the wooden shed against the end wall. Wooden fencing 1.8m (6ft) high marks the boundaries. A camellia grows against the fence to the east. The only access is through the house, using the French windows in the sitting room.

The new garden has been designed as an extension of the home, to provide a safe play space for small children and an interesting outlook from the house, with the provision for eating outside when the weather allows.

To eliminate the slope, the garden was divided into two levels (the upper and lower terraces) by a low wall with steps for access.

BELOW *For small garden owners who are determined to include a water feature, a wall fountain makes good use of the available space.*

POINTS TO CONSIDER

- Small lawns can be difficult to mow and town gardens frequently suffer from a lot of shade, so it is often a good idea to remove the lawn completely and expand the terrace.
- Pots of annuals add extra colour to even the smallest garden and last from late spring until the first frosts.
- When constructing a paved area, use small paving units to make the garden look larger.

Both terraces were paved with frost-proof terracotta tiles, similar in size and colour to those used in the sitting room and kitchen. They were laid to a slight cross-fall, to drain rainwater on to the planted areas to the west. The boundary fences followed the original slope, so planted areas were left on either side of the paving, which could be sloped to avoid creating a gap at the bottom of the fence.

UPPER AND LOWER TERRACES

The lower terrace was designed to create the maximum room for play equipment. A purpose-built sandpit was positioned in full view of the kitchen window and a bench placed in the shade of a small tree. There are two positions for the table and chairs — when they are by the water feature, an inflatable paddling pool will fit beside the sandpit on the lower terrace.

The upper terrace is designed to form an attractive view from the house with a lion's head wall fountain providing a focal point. The shed is painted bright blue to provide a colourful contrast to the terracotta tiles. It is used for storage but it could be cleared and used as a playhouse for the children when they are older. Containers of bedding plants provide extra colour, with lobelia and marigolds in summer, and blue pansies and orange tulips in the spring.

The whole garden is paved with terracotta tiles, to match those in the adjacent sitting room.

A low wall with off-centre steps divides the garden. The wall is an ideal height – 35cm (14in) – for providing extra seating.

A selection of culinary herbs and a bay tree are planted close to the kitchen.

Two positions are given for the table and chairs, which have to stay out all year as there is no inside storage room.

The sandpit is built into the terrace. It is fitted with a cover to keep cats out.

A small shed has been painted in a bright colour so that it is attractive when viewed from the house. It is lockable and can be used for storage.

Lion's head wall fountain. The water falls into a raised pool filled with pebbles.

ABOVE This is a plan for a small, enclosed garden behind a terraced house in the middle of a large town. The garden is 9m x 5m (28ft x 16ft), and slopes slightly towards the house. The only access is through the French windows. The owners are a young couple with a two-year-old child and a new baby.

31

CREATING YOUR GARDEN

2

Now that you have decided on the type of garden you want, this is the time to make practical choices. Garden furniture comes in many shapes and sizes, and play items such as swings and climbing frames need careful thought. Do you want a perfect lawn or one that will withstand football games? Do you prefer paving, brickwork, gravel or decking, and would you like to include a wildlife pond or a wall fountain? This section will provide you with all the information you need to make the right choices for your garden.

LEFT *The creation of a relatively secluded area, where it is possible to relax in peace, might be a priority in a large, noisy household.*

GARDEN FURNITURE • CHOICES

❶

TABLE AND CHAIRS

If you plan to eat out in the garden, you will need to consider a table and enough chairs to have one for each member of the family. Decide if you want them to stay out all year or whether they will be brought in either at night or for the winter. The choice is vast, but look for sturdy chairs that will not tip over when stood on by an active toddler.

If the family enjoys lying about in the garden, sunbathing, sleeping or reading, then it may be worth investing in a couple of loungers. These can be simple aluminium folding sunbeds or more sophisticated sun loungers with adjustable feet and backs so that you can get really comfortable. They are made of wood, plastic or resin, and usually come with fitted cushions that can be removed.

CHOICE CHECKLIST	
❧ Consider comfort and durability first and buy the best quality that you can afford. ❧ All furniture needs to be checked regularly for loose	bolts and screws and cracked legs and seats. ❧ Plastic is generally cheap, light and easy to move about, but may discolour and become brittle with age.

❷

BENCHES

These are seats for two or three people to sit on, and they are usually made of wood or metal. Metal seats can look very attractive, but wood is much warmer and softer to sit on. Perfect as seats placed around the garden in the sun or shade, they should be carefully sited to create attractive pictures – under a tree, at the end of a path, or beneath a rose arch, for example.

Picnic benches are rectangular tables with benches built in on either side. They are usually made of solid wood and can be heavy to lift and move. Lighter-weight versions and smaller models for children to use are now available. They can be used on the terrace but are more suitable for casual use, and are best placed in a long grass area.

CHOICE CHECKLIST	
❧ Traditional stone benches are elegant but expensive and uncomfortable to sit on. ❧ Wooden benches come in a range of prices and are comfortable, look natural and	will last a long time if regularly oiled or painted. ❧ Painted metal can look attractive and is durable but will need regular repainting and can be uncomfortable.

❸

HAMMOCKS AND SWING SEATS

A hammock stretched out between two trees invites you to climb in and relax as it gently sways. Made in a variety of soft but strong materials, they are now available with either one or two supports for use when either a single tree or no other support is available. For young children, hammocks could form part of a make-believe game of pirates and shipwrecks, while older family members will simply enjoy the relaxing experience.

A more expensive, but extremely comfortable, alternative is a cushioned swing seat, which is much easier to get into and out of than a hammock, particularly for an older member of the family. Swing seats usually have a canopy at the top of the frame, so an added bonus is shade from the sun.

CHOICE CHECKLIST

✎ Most hammocks are made of rot-proof materials which can be left outside all summer without damage.
✎ Check that there is adequate space for swinging without hitting anything.
✎ Hammocks require secure and robust fixtures and swing seat frames need to be correctly anchored to the ground.

❹

LOGS AS FURNITURE

There are lots of inexpensive or even free ways of furnishing a garden, particularly where children are concerned. A few large logs cut to the right length and stood upright are instant stools, and if a larger slab of wood is laid on three or four of the logs, you have a rustic table. A large log left lying on its side makes a comfortable child-height bench. If you are feeling imaginative, and have some carpentry skills, you could construct a table and some chairs … or even a tree-house!

If there are large smooth rocks, they can also be used as chairs and tables, but be sure they are set firmly into the ground. Remember that rocks will be slippery when wet, so discourage young children from clambering on them after rain.

CHOICE CHECKLIST

✎ Use hardwood logs where available as these take longer to rot than softwood.
✎ Check logs for loose splinters and remove any before placing in position.
✎ Logs will attract insects so avoid using them if your children dislike creepy-crawlies (though these will provide a source of interest for some children).

PLAYING IN THE GARDEN • CHOICES

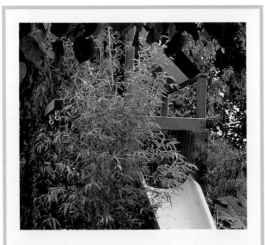

❶

SWINGS AND SLIDES

A simple wooden swing or rubber tyre suspended from a tree branch or frame is still a firm favourite with all age groups. Make the swing sturdy enough, and even adults may be found idly swinging backwards and forwards when no one is looking. Purpose-built swings can be made that have room for plants like honeysuckle to be planted over them to make a very attractive garden feature.

Slides come in a variety of materials, but safety remains a major consideration. A slide should have handrails at the top and high enough sides to prevent children falling out. The safest slide is one that follows the contours of a slope. Consider buying a plastic slide for a toddler and a larger slide for older children that will last for many years.

CHOICE CHECKLIST	
❧ Slides need a clear space at the bottom where children can land. ❧ Wood looks more natural in the garden than the plastic alternatives.	❧ Swings need space in front and behind to ensure that nobody gets hit when the swing is in motion.

❷

CLIMBING FRAMES

Children love climbing, whether it is ropes, ladders, rocks or trees. A strong tree with plenty of low branches will make the perfect climbing frame, and nothing else is really necessary. If, however, you hang a rope ladder from one branch, a swing from another, and place a simple platform in a fork in the tree, you have a ready-made adventure playground. If you do not have a suitable tree, you will need some form of framework, metal or wood, to which ropes, rope ladders, scrambling nets or solid ladders can be fixed. The same structure can be used to support a slide, a swing and even a platform with a roof, which can be used as a playhouse. Never site a climbing frame on a hard surface: choose grass or lay a safety surface.

CHOICE CHECKLIST	
❧ Any climbing equipment needs clear space at the base for jumping off safely. ❧ Check all fittings and fixtures regularly for signs of wear.	❧ Choose a system that allows attachments to be altered as children get older, for example, being able to change a baby swing for a rubber tyre swing.

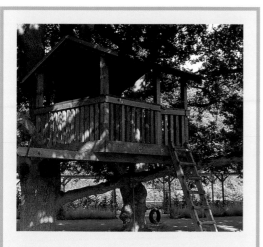

❸

PLAYHOUSES

Playhouses, hideouts, tree-houses and dens are all spaces for children to use where they can enter their own world of make-believe. Where a more permanent dwelling is wanted, look for a structure that will be strong and big enough for several years of play. A well-built wooden house may be more expensive than a plastic one, but it will give years of pleasure. An ordinary garden shed, with the addition of a child-sized door and small windows, can make a dream cottage that can be returned to its original function when no longer needed. Playhouses are best as a permanent fixture in the garden, and can form an attractive picture. You could enhance the view by adding a garden around the sides or placing flower pots in front.

CHOICE CHECKLIST

❧ The adjacent garden and pots could be planted by the user or users of the playhouse and be their special responsibility.

❧ Large cardboard boxes, suitably painted and with holes cut out for windows and doors, make great temporary houses and can be thrown away afterwards.

❹

FLOORING FOR PLAYSPACES

For toys that are put away at night, grass makes the perfect flooring as it is soft and resilient to play on. Where play equipment is to be fixed permanently, grass is less satisfactory as it tends to get worn and muddy. The grass may be difficult to mow and, if the play equipment is in shade, will not grow well. Sand is used in some children's playgrounds, because it is soft to fall on and can be used for digging, but more often nowadays you find a specially laid safety surface. For the garden, bark chippings are a good choice: they will provide a cushion on which to fall, and their natural dark colour blends well with beds and borders. Another alternative is to lay an area of rubber safety tiles, which have the added advantage of being washable.

CHOICE CHECKLIST

❧ There is a wide range of grades of bark chippings available. It is important to choose a non-splintery bark for playgrounds – you may need professional advice.

❧ Before laying any surface, check that the soil beneath is well drained to prevent water-logging.
❧ Rubber tiles are a good choice but can be expensive.

PAVING MATERIALS • CHOICES

❶

PAVING SLABS

Natural stone slabs are made from quarried sand-stone, slate or limestone. They look lovely but are expensive, heavy to handle and lay, and most can be slippery when wet.

Reconstituted stone slabs are pre-cast slabs made from crushed stone mixed with a binding of cement; they come in a wide variety of shapes, colours, sizes and finishes. All good garden centres have a selection on display, and many of the companies supplying the slabs have excellent catalogues that give instructions for laying them.

Finally, concrete slabs are strong, durable and cheap but rather dull and uninteresting. If this is the only choice available or affordable, then add interest with an edging of paving blocks or bricks.

CHOICE CHECKLIST	
❧ Select slabs to match materials already used in the garden or in the house. ❧ Ensure that all paved surfaces are laid to a minimum fall of 1 in 100	away from the house or garden walls. ❧ The level of the terrace should be at least 15cm (6in) below the damp-proof membrane of the house.

❷

BRICK PAVERS AND PAVING BLOCKS

Brick pavers are clay bricks similar to house bricks but often thinner and without a recess on one side. They can be found to match the colour of many house and walling bricks, and are most attractive in a garden. Available as both reclaimed and new, they are excellent for paths or detailing to concrete and paving slabs, but rather uncomfortable as the sole material for a terrace. They are also expensive and can be rather slippery when covered with moss.

Paving blocks are durable units, about the same size as a brick, made from clay or concrete. They are available in a wide range of colours and some unusual shapes, with either straight or bevelled edges. Frequently used on drives, they are fairly expensive to buy and time-consuming to lay.

CHOICE CHECKLIST	
❧ There are many different patterns for laying bricks – select the pattern most suitable for the area. ❧ Check that any bricks used for paving are frostproof	– bricks used in walls may not be and will break up in a cold winter. ❧ Large areas of bricks can look 'busy' so break them up with larger paving units.

❸

DECKING

Wooden decking and tiles have been used for many years in countries with dry climates. Despite being slippery when wet, wooden tiles are now gaining in popularity as they tend to look softer and more natural in a garden setting than the stone alternatives. Decking can be used to replace a terrace, as a surround for a pond, or anywhere in the garden where you want a low platform.

Good decking is expensive but worth the cost; cheaper versions are rather splintery for knees and bare feet. Avoid mixing decking with other paving material such as stone slabs as it can look rather untidy. The only surface material with which it associates well is loose stone, whether gravel, pebbles, cobbles or even large rocks and boulders.

CHOICE CHECKLIST	
❧ Choose the best quality decking that you can afford. ❧ Avoid laying decking on bare soil – use battens of treated timber as a support.	❧ Decking is lightweight and ideal for roof gardens. ❧ You can use decking as an elegant method for covering up expanses of ugly concrete.

❹

GRAVEL AND CONCRETE

Gravel is by far the cheapest material to use for drives or garden paths and includes a wide range of small stones from angular chippings to rounded pea shingle. It is a useful material for less formal parts of the garden and combines well with rocks and water features. The finer the gravel the easier it is to walk on, and there is a self-binding gravel which makes a compacted, hard-wearing surface. Gravel is not suitable for a terrace and should only be used for paths if there are no small children.

Concrete is often considered too utilitarian for a garden, but it makes a perfect, smooth bicycle track or hard play area. If used for a path, it will look much more attractive if given a brick or block-paving edging.

CHOICE CHECKLIST	
❧ Look at a range of gravel sizes and colours before making your selection. ❧ Gravel can be laid on a geo-textile membrane to suppress weeds.	❧ Concrete can be coloured and can be laid with an extensive range of different finishes including smooth, brushed or exposed aggregate.

WATER FEATURES • CHOICES

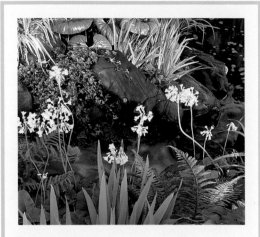

①

PEBBLE FOUNTAINS

There are several different styles of pebble fountain but they all consist of a sunken reservoir containing water and a pump. The reservoir is covered with a lid or mesh on which are placed large pebbles. A jet of water rises out of the pebbles, and the water falls back through the stones and into the reservoir. In some versions, the jet comes up and over a millstone that sits on the pebbles.

Installing jets in paving is basically a more sophisticated version of the pebble fountain, where the lid supports paving rather than pebbles. Jets of water shoot up through the paving and then drain back through gaps into the reservoir. Children can run through the jets, and there is the potential to have a hidden switch to turn them on and off.

CHOICE CHECKLIST	
❧ An excellent choice where small children are concerned as there is no exposed body of water. ❧ Available in a wide range of sizes and styles and	suitable for even the smallest of gardens. ❧ Include as large a reservoir as possible to avoid endless refilling.

②

SHALLOW STREAM

A less obvious idea, but one ideal for children's games, is to create a water feature that is filled only when needed and left empty when not in use. A shallow indentation or ditch is excavated as part of the terrace, and then a hard surface material is laid. Small unit paving, setts and bricks are all suitable, but they must be properly laid with mortared joints, and the levels must be right. A hose can be used to fill the channel when a stream is wanted, and a temporary dam placed at the end of the channel can be removed when play has finished. The stream can double as a drainage channel for the terrace – but it is important to plan the stream as part of the pattern of the terraced area to ensure that it is visually appealing when empty.

CHOICE CHECKLIST	
❧ Safe except for very small children. ❧ Easy to maintain and keep clean. ❧ Good value for paddling, boats and water play.	❧ Needs careful planning. ❧ Allow a slight slope – at least 1 in 100 – to ensure that the stream drains completely when not in use.

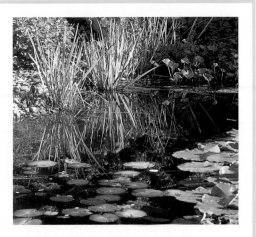

❸

WALL FOUNTAIN AND RAISED POND

This attractive feature comes in a wide variety of designs and prices, ranging from a simple jet falling into a basin to a series of elaborate jets falling into a large raised pool. Where the basin or pool is large enough, aquatic plants and fish may be introduced into the water. Choose according to site, preference and budget.

The pond height needs to be a minimum of 40cm (14in) which will prevent small children or others from tripping over the edge and still allow everyone to view the pond easily. Up to 50cm the edge of the pond can be used as a sitting area by adults and children. If there are very young children, select a wall fountain which falls into a high bowl fixed to the wall well out of reach.

CHOICE CHECKLIST	
❧ Ensure that there is a nearby water supply to allow regular refilling.	❧ It is possible to buy a kit which includes the pool, jets and pump.
❧ Fountains can be very ornamental and give pleasure to all the family.	❧ Ensure that the pipe from the pool to the wall fountain is completely obscured.

❹

GROUND-LEVEL POOL

Ground-level pools, whether formal or informal, are the most popular of all water features, and will appeal to young and old alike. They give the opportunity to grow various water and bog plants, and will attract many kinds of wildlife.

They can be installed easily using a pre-formed shell or, more inexpensively, a butyl liner. Decide on the position for the pool and its shape, then dig out the soil to the required depth. Cover the base and sides with a layer of padding, then carefully fit the liner. Fill the pool with water so that the liner is fully stretched into the contours of the pool, then edge the pool with paving. This will hide the top of the pond liner and makes an attractive feature in its own right.

CHOICE CHECKLIST	
❧ A fountain can be added for extra interest or even a waterfall.	❧ A method of controlling algae needs to be considered before selecting this type of water feature.
❧ Pools can be planted with a range of attractive water plants.	❧ Can be as small or large as space allows.

USE OF GRASS AREAS • CHOICES

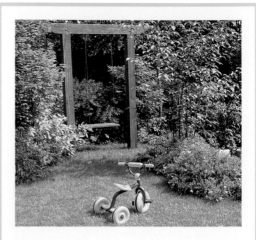

❶

LUXURY LAWN

This is the perfect lawn, with a smooth, velvety green sward and the typical stripes of precision mowing. It is the result of a mixture of fine grasses and close and regular mowing with a cylinder mower. This lawn looks extremely beautiful but needs very careful preparation and constant care and allows little or no wear. It is therefore not really suitable for a family garden unless one of the family is a lawn 'fanatic', and would certainly not be the right choice if anyone wanted to play football or tennis or ride a bike on it. This is a lawn for admiring from afar rather than using. For a more practical lawn that allows occasional wear, add 40% creeping red fescue and reduce the Chewings fescue to 40%.

❷

UTILITY LAWN

This is a useful lawn for a family garden; fine grasses mixed with perennial rye grass give a smooth, green sward that will take the pressures of everyone walking over it and the odd football game. The perennial rye grass is quick to germinate and resistant to wear, but it will not tolerate being cut too short. There are enough fine grasses in the mixture to give the appearance of a neatly mown lawn.

Ground preparation is essential for a good quality lawn. Ensure that all perennial weeds have been removed, and, if possible, leave the prepared soil for a few weeks before sowing so that any remaining weed seeds have time to germinate. Spring is the ideal time to sow a new lawn; if you are not ready to sow then, wait until autumn.

CHOICE CHECKLIST

- Seed mixture should be 80% Chewings fescue and 20% browntop bent.
- Mow when grass reaches 6–12mm (¼–½in) high.
- Mow at least once a week in summer.
- Scarify and feed the lawn each spring and re-seed bare areas if, and when, they appear.

CHOICE CHECKLIST

- Seed mixture should be 30% perennial rye grass, 30% creeping red fescue, 25% Chewings fescue, 10% smooth-stalked meadow grass and 5% browntop bent.
- Mow once a week when grass reaches a height of 12–18mm (½–¾in).

❸

PLAY AREAS

This grass area is intended for regular use and the hard wear of vigorous ball games and being covered with paddling pools and tents, or more permanently with play equipment. The grass mixture may include a much larger proportion of perennial rye grass which will put up with the continuous pressure of feet. The grass is cut at a higher level and is difficult to keep looking well groomed.

Weeds may be a problem as the higher level of mowing allows ground-hugging plants like plantains, daisies and buttercups to grow undisturbed. Hand weeding or use of a selective weedkiller may be needed to keep them under control. When the area gets damaged it is very easy to re-seed as perennial rye grass germinates very rapidly.

CHOICE CHECKLIST

❧ Try a seed mixture of 60% perennial rye grass, 35% creeping red fescue and 5% browntop bent.
❧ Mow when the grass has reached 25mm (1in).

❧ Check for toys and remove before mowing as they can seriously damage mower blades.

❹

WILD FLOWER MEADOW

A meadow is a lovely idea but not easy to establish, because the grass tends to take over from the wild flowers. Choose an area where the topsoil is poor, because this will inhibit grass growth and give the wild flowers a chance to get established. Sow seeds of wild flowers with the grasses, or plant small plants (plugs) of the wild flowers once the grass is established. Cut with a rotary mower.

An alternative is to plant bulbs in the grass and leave them to naturalize. The grass is mown in the late autumn and then left for the bulbs to appear in spring. Mowing is then delayed until the bulbs have died down in late spring. Seed mixtures can include a wide range of grasses, but not perennial rye grass because it is much too vigorous.

CHOICE CHECKLIST

❧ Try a mix of 40% creeping red fescue, 20% Chewings fescue, 25% hard fescue, 10% smooth-stalked meadow grass and 5% browntop bent.

❧ For a longer lawn, try a mix of 45% hard fescue, 30% crested dog's tail, 10% Timothy, 8% smooth-stalked meadow grass and 7% browntop bent.

GARDEN BASICS

A new garden will almost certainly need some plants, and most of these may need to be purchased from a suitable supplier. Try to decide what you want before you go, using the plant directory on pages 64 to 99 to tell you which plants will be suitable for your garden. If you buy on impulse, you risk being disappointed when your sun-loving purchase fails to flourish in your shady garden.

Plants are available for sale in a variety of outlets, from specialist nurseries and garden centres to the local greengrocer, market stall or garage. Nurseries usually grow and sell their own plants, but, although the staff are usually very knowledgeable and helpful about the plants they grow, they may not have all the plants you are seeking. Most garden centres carry a whole range of plants from large conifers to tiny alpines, and some will look for plants from other sources when requested. When making a list of the plants you want, always put down the Latin name because most nurseries and garden centres arrange their plants alphabetically by their Latin names.

The best time to plant trees, shrubs and roses is in the dormant season in winter, and this is also a good time to buy these plants. Herbaceous plants and conifers, by contrast, are best bought and planted in autumn or spring.

Although plants in containers can be planted at any time of the year, the top buying and planting season is Easter to early summer. Planting in the spring means that the plant will go into soil that is beginning to warm up; and, if kept well watered in dry periods, it should start to grow immediately and continue to grow all summer.

BUYING BULBS

Spring-flowering bulbs are usually planted in September and October, although they are on sale from late August onwards. Garden centres carry a good range of standard varieties at reasonable prices, but a much wider range can be found through mail-order specialist bulb companies. Their catalogues come out in midsummer, and orders are sent out in August and September. Summer- and autumn-flowering bulbs are usually planted in the spring and are available for sale in the late winter. Always check the planting time when buying bulbs, because they are best planted as soon as possible after buying or delivery.

BUYING SEEDS

Seeds can be bought in garden centres from late winter onwards for early spring sowing. Again, there are specialist seed firms that supply a much wider range of seeds, but you need to allow time for your order to be processed and there may be a charge for delivery. The number of seeds in a packet varies widely, but it is often printed on the packet or in the seed catalogue, so you can check that a packet contains enough before you buy. Seeds will keep for some time but need to be stored in a dark, dry place. Some seeds come in foil inner packets which allow easier resealing when necessary. These packets are particularly useful with some salad crops that are to be sown in succession. If a seed packet contains more than you need, share them with your friends rather than keeping them until the next year.

LEFT With careful advance planning, you can ensure colour in the garden in every season.

HINTS AND TIPS

🌿 Make a list and set yourself a budget before buying plants – it is very easy to get carried away when faced with a garden centre full of lots of lovely plants!

🌿 Many nurseries have reference books available for customers' use, so if you see a plant that looks fascinating but you know nothing about it, look it up before buying.

🌿 Always check that the soil, light and moisture requirements of the plants you buy match the conditions in your garden. It is very, very easy to see an attractive plant but not note that it requires an acid soil and deep shade whilst you have a chalk garden in full sunlight.

🌿 Do not be seduced by plants in flower. The best plant to buy is one that is growing vigorously, and that is usually before it is in flower. However, if you are looking for a particular colour within a species, it is safest to choose a plant whose flowers are out, otherwise you could get a disappointing surprise.

🌿 Look for lots of healthy shoots and young leaves about to open. Dead leaves and shoots indicate a plant that is under stress.

TECHNIQUE   SELECTING PLANTS IN CONTAINERS

1 The compost in the container must be moist without being waterlogged. If it is excessively wet, the roots may have started to rot. If it has dried out the plant may die.

2 If moss is present on the surface of the compost, this indicates that the plant has been neglected and has been in the pot too long.

3 Check that masses of roots are not protruding out of the container's drainage holes. This indicates that the plant is pot bound. Plants seldom fully recover if the roots are excessively matted.

4 Check that the plant has not been recently potted up for a quick sale. Reputable suppliers will not try to hoodwink potential customers, as this state often cannot be detected until the plant is planted. Make sure too that the plant is clearly labelled.

INCREASING PLANTS

If you are given plants, check that there are no signs of disease before you plant them in your garden. If you are given cuttings, keep them in water in a plastic bag until you are ready to handle them, then dip the stem of each cutting in hormone rooting powder or liquid, and plant in some cutting compost. Water them gently. You can put quite a few cuttings into one pot. Cover them with a plastic bag (sealed round the pot with a rubber band), which forms a cocoon over the plants to keep the moisture in. The bag must not touch the leaves of the cuttings, or they will turn brown and drop off. If your cuttings start to go mouldy, then they are probably too damp: you need to clear the accumulated moisture off the inside of the bag at regular intervals.

If you have a friend with a herbaceous plant that needs dividing, this is an excellent way to add to your own garden. The plant needs to be dug up carefully, by inserting two garden forks, back to back, into the centre of the clump, gently levering the plant in half. The centre of the plant will often be woody, so the division of the plant should be continued until sufficient pieces have been removed from the outside. The centre should be discarded, and the outside pieces are then ready for replanting.

CARE AND MAINTENANCE

The whole idea of this book is to keep garden maintenance to a minimum to allow all members of the family to enjoy the garden. However, plants are living organisms and will need a little help to keep them alive and well. The secret to a healthy garden is a good humus-rich soil and plants that have been selected for the specific soil, moisture and sunlight conditions found in the bed in which they are planted. Strong growing plants are less likely to succumb to the various pests and diseases commonly affecting garden plants.

Whichever type of lawn or grass area you decide to include in your garden, it will require regular maintenance. Wild flower meadows may need mowing only twice a year and should never be fed, but a quality lawn needs spiking, feeding, as well as mowing once a week in summer.

One of the more common problems suffered by lawns in family gardens is the grass dying in small areas – frequent games of football, or leaving a paddling pool too long in one place, are the quickest ways to end up with bald patches on the lawn.

WILD FLOWER MEADOWS

However small the garden, if there is room for a lawn, then it is worth keeping part of the grass area as a wild flower meadow. The grass is left uncut in spring to allow other plants, such as daisies, dandelions, yarrow, plantains and other wild flowers to grow. Children and adults alike will enjoy this area. Many of these flowers are also useful caterpillar plants and will help to attract butterflies into your garden. However, if anyone in the family is a hay fever sufferer, a wild flower meadow may not be a good idea.

TECHNIQUE   **REPAIRING BARE PATCHES IN THE LAWN**

1 Remove the dead grass and gently fork the affected area using a hand or garden fork, depending on the size of the area.

2 Rake the surface of the soil and remove any debris, checking that the surface of the soil is level with the surrounding grass. Add additional sieved topsoil if needed.

3 Rake to form a fine seed bed and sow grass seed at 30g per sq. m (1oz per sq. yd). See pages 42 and 43.

4 Cover the seed with a thin layer of sieved soil and press down with a board.

5 Water with a fine rose on a hose or watering can, being careful not to disturb the seed.

6 Protect from children and birds with crossed strands of thread.

1 Allocate a minimum space of 1 x 1m (39 x 39in) for the compost heap. A concrete or paved base makes it easier to remove the compost, but level, compacted soil is just as good, and also contains heat.

2 Make a bunker with wooden or brick sides and an open front. Place hedge clippings, cabbage leaves or other coarse material at the bottom of the heap to allow air to get in and help the decaying process.

3 Place a layer of mixed garden waste on the heap; kitchen vegetable waste, lawn clippings, annual weeds, dead leaves and flower heads can all be included, but avoid any plants containing seeds.

4 Add some soil to the heap if none is present in the garden waste; also a little nitrogen-rich fertilizer (both encourage bacteria). Water the heap in dry weather.

5 Keep adding layers of vegetable waste, soil and fertilizer until the heap is about 1m (39in) high. Cover with some extra soil and, in cold weather, with newspaper.

6 After 6–12 weeks you should have a brown crumbly compost. Remove the top and use as the base of the next compost heap; use the rest on the garden.

Some of these plants will occur naturally and some can be planted, including oxeye daisies, ragged robins, cowslips, knapweed and harebells.

The area needs to be cut after the flowers are over in July: the grass can then be left to grow and should be mown only once a month to the end of autumn. This longer grass is softer to sit on and is perfect for picnics and campsites.

GRASS PATHS

Mown grass paths are a sensible, low-cost choice of path for less formal areas of the garden and for any path that is not used all the time. Use the utility lawn grass mixture *(see page 42)* and mow when the main lawn is mown. They need to be planned to be wide enough to allow easy access around the garden and to make mowing easy.

🌢 In the first spring and summer after planting, all plants will need regular watering during dry periods.

🌢 A check needs to be kept for weeds and these removed as soon as they appear, to avoid becoming a problem.

🌢 Deadhead flowers, as this usually results in more vigorous plant growth as well as making the plant look more attractive.

🌢 Most plants will benefit from an annual feed in the spring with a balanced fertilizer containing equal amounts of nitrogen, phosphates and potassium.

🌢 An annual mulch of composted organic matter applied to the surface of the soil will keep the soil rich in humus, which is formed as the organic matter breaks down in the soil. The best source of this is garden-made compost from the compost heap.

SAFETY IN THE GARDEN

*F*amily gardens should be, first and foremost, spaces in which the whole family can relax and enjoy themselves. For parents to be fully relaxed, they need to be certain that their offspring are safe and that they have guarded against all possible dangers. However, the need for safety will vary with the age of the children using the garden, and will change as children grow older.

A totally safe garden would be a space surrounded by high smooth walls and with a floor of washable rubber tiles on which were placed a few plastic toys. This might be fine for babies and toddlers, but would be a sterile desert to an adventurous older child. At the other extreme, a garden with no boundaries, deep pools of water with steep drops into fast-flowing streams, uneven, slippery paving, lots of poisonous plants and an old greenhouse with rotten glazing bars and broken glass is a gloriously exciting place but a potential danger for every member of the family.

So how safe should your garden be? Look at what might constitute specific dangers for members of your family and then consider how to minimize those dangers. Get the older members of the family to do a risk assessment of your garden, as this will get them to appreciate the dangers for themselves and make them aware of how to avoid any potential problems.

BELOW *The flush edge to this relatively deep pool would be unsafe for small children.*

POINTS TO CONSIDER

RISK ASSESSMENT
Risk assessment means taking a potential hazard and looking at it in terms of the following:

- How likely is it to cause an accident?
- High chance /some chance /low chance
- How serious would the effect be?
- Death /serious injury /slight injury
- What could be done to minimize the risk?
- If there is a high chance of a serious accident and there is a way of minimizing the risk, then this should be done.

Examples of garden pitfalls for an active two-year-old include the following:

Easily opened gate to road
- High chance of running out into road and traffic.
Action – Replace gate immediately.

Open pond on terrace
- High chance of slipping and falling in.
- Possibility of drowning.
- Could fence pond (unsightly), watch child constantly (not realistic) or replace pond with paving.
Action – Replace pond with paving.

Mildly poisonous aquilegia in front of border
- No bright berries, so low chance of child being attracted to eating the plant.
- Would cause stomach ache if eaten, but this is not dangerous.
Action – Lift aquilegia and replant in middle or back of border.

RISKS FOR CHILDREN

Children have little sense of danger and are therefore most vulnerable to accidents, so while they are small there are a number of things you can do to make the garden safer.

�añ Fence or remove open water – small children can drown in a few centimetres of water.

�añ Ensure that children are always visible when playing in the garden by avoiding features that obscure parts of the view.

�añ Check for poisonous plants – some children put everything into their mouths, and older children may mistake poisonous fruit for cherries or blackcurrants. Remove all very poisonous plants (see entries on pages 104 to 107 of the plant directory).

�añ Check on plants that can cause skin rashes and allergies and decide whether to remove any present in the garden (see entries on pages 100 and 101 of the directory).

�añ Position play equipment carefully so that children on swings cannot hit anything or anybody; and ensure that slides have protected tops. Always carefully follow the manufacturer's instructions for assembly and anchorage.

�añ Select soft material for the base of play equipment, either grass, bark, mulch, sand or rubber tiles, so that if a child falls the result is not too serious.

RISKS FOR ALL THE FAMILY

There are some potential hazards in a garden that might be dangerous for any family member, whatever their age and agility, and care needs to be taken with the following:

�añ Avoid sharp objects – check for possible dangers like broken glass and projecting edges in greenhouses; ground-floor windows that open onto paths and terraces; sharp corners of coping on walls.

�añ Cover tops of plant stakes and bamboos with rubber tips to avoid jabbing eyes or limbs when gardening.

�añ Consider the position of plants with sharp thorns or prickles (see entries on pages 102 and 103 of the directory) and remove any of these plants that are adjacent to paths and children's play areas.

�añ Create sitting and playing areas in shade to prevent sunburn.

�añ Check and re-lay uneven and broken paving – this is dangerous to all members of the family but particularly the very young and the elderly.

�añ Ensure that all garden chemicals and tools are kept in a locked shed and that the key is accessible only to responsible members of the family.

�añ Have a well-equipped first aid kit in the house and be sure that all members of the family know where it is kept.

ELECTRICITY

There are obvious dangers in using electricity in the garden, so take special care with equipment and electrically operated garden features, such as pumps on fountains.

�añ All garden supplies must be fitted with a circuit breaker. Seek advice from a qualified electrician.

�añ All electric cables must be armoured to protect them from accidental damage.

�añ Carry out regular checks on all electrical equipment, and replace any worn or damaged parts.

THE CARE AND USE OF TOOLS

Always put garden tools away after use in a locked shed, and note these other points about their safe use:

�añ Learn how to dig properly to avoid damaging your back, and teach children to do the same.

�añ When using tools, always place them so that they are safe, e.g. do not leave a rake with its teeth facing upwards.

USE AND STORAGE OF CHEMICALS

Most of us would probably prefer not to use any chemicals in the garden, but they are useful aids and frequently there will be a few garden chemicals that need storing in your lockable garden shed. Here are a few additional rules:

�añ Always read the instructions and follow them.

�añ Never remove or destroy labels.

�añ Never change containers, e.g. never pour weedkiller into an old lemonade bottle.

�añ Never keep made-up solutions for use later.

�añ Safely dispose of out-of-date or unused chemicals – contact your local authority for disposal advice.

�añ Buy chemicals only when you are sure you need them and use them immediately.

PLANTING THE FAMILY GARDEN

*I*n a small garden, plant trees, shrubs, climbers and some of the tougher border plants that *everybody can enjoy, and then add extra, perhaps more exciting, plants when the children have grown up and left home. Using child-resistant plants does not mean missing out on colour and interest — there are lots of lovely plants that are tough and easy to grow, which are detailed in the plant directory, and in the star plants box on this page.*

The most frequently made mistake in tree selection is choosing too large a tree so that, just as it matures into a really lovely specimen, it grows too large and has to be

chopped down or pruned back. Trees should offer year-round interest if possible, or at least an extended season of interest. In the plant directory there are 12 trees that are selected as being easy to grow, including *Sorbus* 'Joseph Rock'. You can buy trees in a variety of sizes from small seedlings to semi-mature 'giants'. The best size for a family garden is a 10–12cm (4–4½in) standard tree. The 10–12cm (4–4½in) is the measurement around the trunk of the tree at 1m (3ft 3in) above the ground, and standard means that the tree will have a clear trunk of 1.8m (6ft) and a well-formed, branching head.

'Bare root' trees are lifted without any soil in the autumn and winter; they should be planted only between late autumn and early spring. 'Container-grown' trees have been grown in a container and are more expensive; these can be planted all year but will need very careful handling and watering if planted in summer.

LEFT *Plant scented roses to fill the garden with perfume. This attractive planting teams them with alchemilla and geraniums.*

PROJECT   **PLANTING A CLIMBER AGAINST A FENCE**

1 Select the position for the climber, perhaps in the middle of a fencing panel or in between panels. Dig a hole 38cm (15in) away from the fence, slightly wider and deeper than the root ball of the climber.

2 Place the container in the hole to check that it is big enough. Fork over the base of the hole and mix in some well-rotted compost. In dry weather, fill the hole with water and let it drain away before planting.

3 Adding water to the hole before planting will ensure that the plant has moisture at its roots. Place the root ball in the hole and fill the gaps with topsoil, making sure that the soil is well firmed in.

4 Push a cane firmly into the soil behind the climber to support the plant and guide it into position. Tie the shoots of the climber loosely to the cane. Water after planting and regularly during the first year.

PROJECT | **PLANTING A BARE ROOT TREE**

1 Select a site for your new tree and place a large cane in the ground to represent the tree. Look at the cane from all parts of the garden and the house to check that the site is correct. Dig a hole roughly 60 x 60 x 60cm (2 x 2 x 2ft), checking that it is large enough to contain the tree roots fully spread out and extra compost at the hole base.

2 Break up the sides and base of the hole by forking before planting to ensure adequate drainage. A newly planted tree requires plenty of water to get it established, but you don't want your tree to be saturated, so drainage is important.

3 Drive the stake in firmly near the centre of the hole so that at least 45cm (18in) of the stake is in the ground and it feels absolutely firm. Position it so that when the tree is placed centrally in the hole the stake will be on the windward side of the tree. Add compost to the soil in the base of the hole.

4 Hold the tree in the hole so that the junction of the roots and trunk of the tree is level with the top of the hole. Gradually fill the hole with soil and compost, making sure that the earth is firmed well down, leaving no air gaps.

5 Tie the tree to the stake at the top and bottom using tree ties (if using a buckled tie make sure the buckle is on the stake and not the tree). The top tie should be nailed to the stake to prevent it slipping down. Water well and then cover the bare soil with 75mm (3in) of bark mulch.

6 Check the tree regularly to see that the stake is not rubbing the tree, and water frequently in dry periods in the first year. The tree ties will need loosening after the first growing season and the stake will need removing as soon as the tree is growing well – usually after three years.

SHRUBS AND HEDGES

Shrubs, particularly evergreen ones, give permanent structure to our gardens as a background to borders, as hedges (both formal and informal), as ground cover and ornamentally as part of a mixed border. Most gardens include a hedge as a boundary, to divide up the garden, or as patterning. A hedge is a row of shrubs planted closely to create a uniform texture; it can be a single or double row. Most shrubs can be used as hedging; some are included in the plant directory *(pages 82 to 85)*.

STAR PLANTS

Some of the best all-round plants for a family garden are:

- *Clematis montana*
- *Hemerocallis* hybrids
- *Malus hupehensis*
- *Penstemon barbatus*
- *Rosa* 'Flower Carpet'
- *Rosa* 'New Dawn'
- *Viburnum tinus*

CHILDREN'S GARDENS

All children should be given the opportunity to grow plants, whether in a flowerpot on the windowsill, in a half barrel on the terrace, or in their own garden. Watching a seed germinate and send out roots and shoots is to watch one of life's wonders, and almost all small children can be encouraged to sow a few seeds.

Start by letting children sow seeds in a pot. Mustard and cress are the quickest seeds to grow, being ready for cutting just two weeks after sowing. Broad beans are fun, as the unfurling leaves are huge; the resulting bean plant can either be left to grow in the pot or planted out in the garden to produce beans. Another favourite use of flowerpots is to have a competition among family members to grow the tallest sunflower. Herbs such as parsley and dill are also useful starter plants for flowerpot growing.

CAPTURING THEIR IMAGINATION

Almost anything can be used as a container– a growbag, an old tyre, old shoes and discarded toys. Whatever container is selected, it must have drainage holes in the base. Once they have grown plants in containers, children may want to have their own patch of garden to try out their new gardening skills and planting ideas.

RIGHT *Strawberry plants are a real winner because they are easy to grow and the fruits are delicious to eat.*

Children should be given an area in which the soil is relatively easy to dig and in which their plants are likely to thrive. An area of heavy clay soil in deep shade will prove

---

PROJECT   **PLANTING A 35CM (14IN) DIAMETER POT OR CONTAINER**

1 Place some broken crocks or stones in the bottom of the container for drainage, and fill the container with fresh planting compost to within 10 cm (4in) of the top.

2 Remove three nicotianas carefully from their pots, and place them close together in the centre of the pot. Press into the compost, adding extra compost between the three plants.

3 Place five petunias equally around the centre plants. Press into the compost, adding extra compost between the petunias and the nicotiana.

4 Place five lobelia and five alyssum alternately around the edge of the pot, and press into the compost. Adjust all the plants to allow equal spacing and then add extra compost. Water with a fine rose on a hose or watering can.

PROJECT | **PETUNIA PIG**

1 Cut an opening in one side of a lemonade bottle large enough to hold five plants, and use a hammer and nails to punch drainage holes in the side of the bottle opposite the opening.

2 Punch a hole in the back of the pig to attach the tail. Cut a piece of felt 10cm (4in) square and then cut it diagonally to make two triangles for the ears. Fold the triangles in half and glue the bottoms together to form the ears. Glue the ears to the bottle.

3 Cut a 5 x 15cm (2 x 6in) piece of felt and wrap it around the pipe cleaner or wire to make the tail. Glue the long edge of the felt to hold it firm. When the glue is dry, coil the tail around a pencil before pushing the end through the tail hole in the bottle. Fix by twisting the end of the tail into a knot.

4 Fill the pig with potting compost, starting with the head and making sure to pack it in well with no large air gaps.

5 Place four corks to form legs and make sure that the pig is steady on its legs before glueing the corks into position. Draw two eyes on the head of the bottle with a black marker pen.

6 Plant the pig with petunias, and water well. Place in a sunny position and water every few days. If you haven't any petunias, any other small plants can be used. You could try sowing grass seeds in the back of the pig; cut your green pig's coat regularly.

daunting to even the most determined young gardener. Assistance from an older member of the family in preparing the soil by digging or rotavating it and in adding plenty of organic matter will help to get the young enthusiast off to a good start.

Encourage children to plan the garden rather than just scatter seeds everywhere. If they have started with container gardening, they may already have strong ideas about the plants they wish to grow. It is their garden, so let them plant every colour together and decorate the garden with whatever they fancy – shells, lengths of wood, plastic toys. Stop a child from expressing their ideas and you may stop them from getting pleasure from the garden. The easiest plants to start with are hardy annuals.

STAR PLANTS

These are some of the best plants for children to grow.

- *Aquilegia vulgaris* (columbine)
- *Calendula officinalis* (marigold)
- *Eschscholzia californica* (Californian poppy)
- *Helianthus annuus* (sunflower)
- *Limnanthes douglasii* (poached egg plant)
- *Nigella damascena* (love-in-a-mist)
- *Tropaeolum majus* (nasturtium)
- *Viola* x *wittrockiana* (pansy)
- Carrots
- Bulbs

WILDLIFE IN THE GARDEN

*M*ost people are fascinated by watching wildlife, whether it be bees busily collecting nectar and pollen, a friendly robin sitting on the fence, or frogs and toads and other watery friends enjoying the garden pond. All of these creatures are a source of endless entertainment and all can be encouraged to come into your garden.

There are over 250 different species of bee living in Britain, including 19 species of the bumble bee. All visit plants to feed on the nectar and collect pollen to feed their young. If you want bees buzzing around your garden, then include some of the plants listed below in your beds and borders. Bees can be seen out foraging almost all year, particularly on warm, sunny days, so plant a range of bee plants that will flower in various seasons.

Butterflies can be attracted into the garden by planting the plants that they are known to visit for nectar. Some of the best butterfly plants are listed below; these can be planted throughout the garden or grouped together to create a butterfly border. Most butterflies are active from mid- to late summer, coinciding with the school summer holidays, and a butterfly bed would make an interesting project for children to plant and maintain themselves.

STAR PLANTS

These are some of the best garden plants for attracting butterflies:

- Aster novi-belgii
- Buddleja davidii
- Centranthus ruber
- Echinops ritro
- Eupatorium cannabinum
- Hebe 'Autumn Glory'
- Origanum laevigatum 'Herrenhausen'
- Sedum spectabile
- Solidago canadensis

Listed here are the best garden plants for attracting bees:

- Borago officinalis
- Cotoneaster horizontalis
- Hyssopus officinalis
- Lavandula angustifolia
- Lythrum salicaria
- Nepeta x faassenii
- Satureja montana
- Ulex europaeus
- Veronica spicata

PROJECT — MAKING A TEMPORARY BIRD HIDE

1 Choose a sheltered part of the garden close to the pond and drive four 2.1m (7ft) posts into the ground to form a 1.2m (4ft) square. Secure four cross pieces to the top of the uprights, to form a square.

2 Create a viewing slit on the side of the hide next to the pond by nailing two cross pieces to the uprights. Nail two pieces of wood vertically between these two horizontals to leave a gap 50cm (20in) wide.

3 Fix sheets of black polythene to the top and three sides of the structure, cutting out a 20 x 50cm (8 x 20in) viewing slit. The side away from the viewing slit should be left uncovered for entry.

4 Camouflage the top and sides of the hide with leafy branches or other foliage. If you use branches of willow or poplar these may root and produce more permanent green cover for your hide.

PROJECT | **PLANTING A BUTTERFLY BORDER**

1 Choose a warm, sheltered part of the garden for the border, which needs to be approximately 2.4m (8ft) wide and 2m (6ft 6in) deep. Dig over the area with a spade to remove any weeds.

2 Spread a thin layer of compost or organic matter over the soil and fork it into the surface.

3 Place a buddleja at the centre back of the border, allowing 1m (3ft 3in) space around it, and then place a solidago and echinops on either side, allowing 60cm (2ft) spacing. When you are satisfied with the spacing, plant the three plants.

4 Now place a hebe and a caryopteris on either side and in front of the buddleja, then add two origanums, one at each end of the middle row, allowing 60cm (2ft) spacing for each of the plants. When you are happy with their positions, plant them carefully.

5 Next plant the front row. Place a sedum in the centre, with two erigeron on one side and two asters on the other. All five plants need 45cm (18in) spacing. Make sure that the plants are 23cm (9in) from the front of the border, then plant carefully.

6 Add annuals such as French marigolds, alyssum and scabious in any gaps in the bed for the first year. Water all the plants thoroughly. In future years when the other plants have started to spread, you may not need to add any annuals.

BIRDS IN THE GARDEN

There are lots of different ways to attract birds to the garden. Rather than planting a specific area for birds, include plants that provide food or nesting material throughout the garden. A source of water can be provided by a bird bath or a water feature, but make sure that there is somewhere flat to perch – a stone in the water is ideal.

Almost all gardens will provide some nesting materials, but you can help by leaving piles of leaves and twigs in the spring and even hanging nets of straw from branches. You could erect a birdbox and hope that a pair of nesting birds will take up residence.

RIGHT *A small copper butterfly collecting nectar from the flowers of* Aster novi-belgii.

VEGETABLES, HERBS AND FRUIT

Freshly picked beans and new potatoes from your own garden are a real delight and are often considered an essential part of the family garden. Indeed some family gardens are given over entirely to the production of food to feed the family.

Whether or not you grow vegetables depends on whether there is a family member who enjoys the work involved. Any activity that is done as a duty and not a pleasure is a chore, and while for a big family with a large garden and a small income, growing food may be essential, other families with smaller gardens should grow vegetables primarily for pleasure. Children enjoy helping to grow vegetables and can be encouraged to sow vegetable seeds in pots. When the seedlings are large enough, they can plant them out in the garden and later have fun harvesting the produce.

In a small garden, container-grown vegetables may be the only option. Fill a terracotta flowerpot with a potting compost that contains some soil, e.g. John Innes potting compost no. 2. Grow different vegetables in separate pots, and provide support when needed: plant runner beans in a large pot and then train them up a trellis tripod.

Another idea when garden space is limited is to grow vegetables in the mixed border. Lettuces, particularly the red-leaved variety 'Red Salad Bowl', make a most attractive edging, and the feathery foliage of carrots is equally suitable for edging a border. Vegetables planted in a border need to be accessible for harvesting their leaves or fruit, so make sure you plant them where they can be reached and not behind a thorny rose or a delicate peony.

PROJECT	MAKING A RUNNER BEAN TEPEE

1 Mark out a circle 1.5m (5ft) in diameter and dig out a trench 10cm (4in) deep. Level the ground and lay out the geo-textile membrane, pushing the extra material into the trench and covering it with soil.

2 Place some tall bamboos around the circle roughly 60cm (2ft) apart, leaving a wider gap for the tepee entrance. Push the bamboos in at an angle, at least 30cm (1ft) into the ground or until they are firm.

3 Tie the bamboos together in the middle with garden twine 15cm (6in) below the top of the poles. Plant a runner bean plant on the outside of each of the poles, and water in well.

4 Sow a circle of carrots around the outside of the runner beans, leaving the entrance to the tepee clear.

5 To protect the beans, tie rows of garden string around the circle of bamboos 5cm (2in), 10cm (4in) and 15cm (6in) up, leaving the entrance clear.

6 Ensure that the beans twine around the poles rather than dangling in mid-air. Add a couple of small paving stones to give dry access to the tepee during showers.

THE VEGETABLE GARDEN

If you want a separate vegetable garden, select a place that is sunny all day and where the soil is deep and fertile. Vegetables are usually grown in straight lines so it helps if the area is regular in shape. Allow room for the compost heap. Traditionally, vegetable gardens had several beds to allow for rotation of crops. If there is room for only a single bed, you will need to be careful about which crops you grow to avoid building up pest and disease problems.

BELOW *Plants for the kitchen can be both productive and decorative. Think also about* *'companion planting' – the use of certain other plants that help to ward off pests.*

FRUIT TREES

Unless you are lucky enough to have a very large garden, there is unlikely to be room for an orchard, but in even the smallest garden there may be space for a cordon fruit tree or two. Cordons have single stems with stubby side branches on which the fruit develop, and both apples and pears can be bought as cordons. They will need to be trained up wires on a wall or trellis, and will require annual pruning to keep them in shape. A single cordon fruit tree can produce up to 2.2kg (5lb) of fruit a year, so even a short row of them should provide the family with plenty of home-grown fruit.

PROJECT CIRCULAR HERB GARDEN

1 Locate the area for your herb circle and then fix a bamboo or peg in the centre. Tie some string loosely to the bamboo or peg, and mark it at 75cm (2ft 6in) from the peg. Walk around the peg keeping the string taut, and mark the radius with sand.

2 Dig the ground within the marked circle thoroughly to remove all existing weeds. Rake the soil roughly level and then mark out the centre slab area and the crossing paths. Remove soil from these areas, then rake and firm the areas by treading.

3 The paths and slab can be laid simply on a bed of sand or, for more stability, on a 7.5cm (3in) layer of stone and mortar with mortared joints.

4 Fork over the areas to be planted and then plant the four herb plants as shown in the diagram. Water in well after planting.

5 Rake a 15cm (6in) wide strip around the edge of the circle and then sow annual herbs in the strip. Cover the seeds with sieved soil and water gently.

6 Complete the garden by adding a pot planted with mint to the centre slab.

A POND FOR WILDLIFE

A pond, however small, introduces a whole new range of wildlife into the garden, from dragonflies and water boatmen to newts, frogs and toads. There is no need to bring in any of these animals — just create a water garden and they will arrive almost overnight.

Ponds naturally occur in hollows in the landscape where water collects and cannot escape, so if there is a low point already in your garden then this is probably the best site for a pond. Otherwise choose a site for your pond bearing in mind the criteria in the box below.

DESIGNING THE POND

An informal shape looks more natural, but if the pond is close to the house you may want a formal design to complement the shape of the house or terrace. Try to keep the shape simple, because complex shapes are difficult to construct and can look awkward. Make sure that there is a gradual slope into the water somewhere so that different animals and birds can reach the water to drink in safety and frogs and toads can climb out.

Part of the pleasure of a wildlife pond is viewing the various inhabitants, so place some stones at the water's edge to allow the family safe and easy access; these stones will also allow birds to get to the water to drink.

PLANTING THE POND

Any pool of water eventually becomes colonized by plants but the first to arrive are algae. In the space of a few days they can turn a pool of clear water into a thick green 'soup'. The best method of controlling the algae is to plant the pond in early summer with a range of plants that will either compete with the algae for food or cover the pool surface with foliage and so deprive the algae of sunlight. A wildlife pond should be planted with native plants rather than exotics, as these are more attractive to native fauna.

There are several different categories of native plants. Oxygenating plants are essential as they live below the surface of the water and compete with the algae for food. They have simple roots and will establish more quickly if planted in water plant containers and placed on the base of the pool rather than simply being dropped into the

LEFT *Pond plants are available from specialist suppliers. They require aquatic compost.*

water. There are several to choose from and it is best to plant a selection.

WATCHPOINTS

🍃 Ponds need to be in sun for most of the day – most water plants prefer full sunlight and shady ponds attract relatively little wildlife.

🍃 Choose a site away from overhanging trees – in autumn the leaves fall into the pond and can cause problems.

🍃 Try to build your pond close to other vegetation – adjacent shrubs, hedges and beds and borders will give cover to small mammals visiting the pond.

🍃 Choose a site sheltered from strong winds.

🍃 Your pond must be sufficiently deep that the water will not freeze solid in winter or overheat in summer – have at least part of the pond a minimum of 60cm (2ft) deep.

Floating aquatic plants float on the surface of the pond and reduce the amount of sunlight reaching the water. This deprives the algae of light and thereby helps to restrict their growth. Check that the floating plants you select are hardy and then place them on the surface of the pond in late spring and leave to grow.

PROJECT	MAKING A WILDLIFE POND USING A LINER

1 Mark out the shape of the pond on the ground, including any areas that are to be used for bog plants.

2 Remove the surface vegetation. If this is grass, lift carefully so that it can be used elsewhere in the garden.

3 Carefully remove the topsoil and store for re-use later.

4 Put in a datum peg to establish the level of the finished pond, then add further pegs around the proposed edge. Use a spirit level and board to ensure that all the pegs are level.

5 Dig out the subsoil to create the pond, allowing for slopes and shelves as planned.

6 Cover the base, sides and shelves with sand or fibre matting to protect the liner from being punctured by stones in the subsoil.

7 Lay the liner over the hole, pulling it taut and placing stones on the edge to hold in position. Make sure that the overlap is evenly distributed.

8 Gradually fill the liner with water so that it stretches to fit the shape of the hole.

9 Cover the edges of the pond with gravel or stones for the sloping beach, paving for the viewing area, and soil for planting areas.

10 Use stored turves to replace any damaged grass areas, and return topsoil to planted areas.

11 Top up water level and add containers of oxygenating, aquatic and marginal plants; place floating plants on the surface of the pond.

12 Plant up any planted areas around the pond.

3

THE PLANT DIRECTORY

This section contains 44 pages of plant entries to help you to select the best plants to grow in your family garden. Apart from the last eight pages, which specify plants to avoid, all the plants selected are those that could be included in your family garden. Whether you are looking for plants for children to grow themselves, a range of easy-to-grow, problem-free plants for the rest of the garden, or plants to eat, they can all be found in the following pages.

LEFT Nepeta x faassenii *(catmint) is planted here to soften the edge of a brick garden path.*

HOW TO USE THIS DIRECTORY

The Plant Directory lists all the plants that are featured in this book, together with a selection of other plants that are suitable for use in a family garden. It is not intended to be exhaustive, and experienced gardeners will have their own favourites. However, this listing has been made with the specific requirements of a family garden in mind, and will guide the beginner to a range of attractive and readily available plants, shrubs and trees with which to create a beautiful garden. Complete information on planting and maintaining the plants is given for each entry.

The Plant Directory is divided into different categories that group like plants together. The categories are annuals and biennials *(page 64)*, bulbs and corms *(page 70)*, herbaceous perennials *(page 72)*, shrubs *(page 82)*, roses *(page 86)*, conifers *(page 87)*, climbers *(page 88)*, trees *(page 90)*, vegetables and fruit *(page 92)*, and herbs *(page 96)*. At the end of the directory there is a listing of plants that are inappropriate for use in a family garden for various reasons. These are grouped together as plants that can cause skin rashes *(page 100)*, plants with thorns and prickles *(page 102)*, and poisonous plants *(page 104)*. The symbols panel accompanying each entry gives essential information on such things as growing conditions, light preference and season of interest.

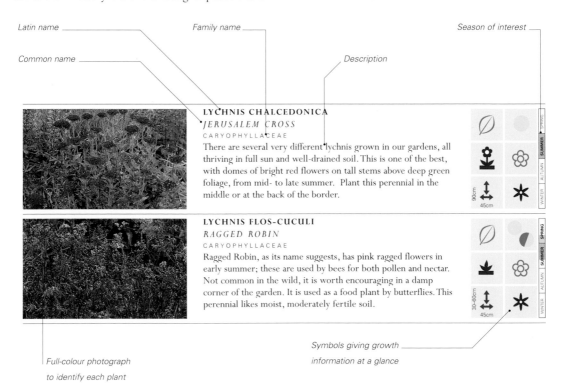

Latin name

Common name

Family name

Description

Season of interest

LYCHNIS CHALCEDONICA
JERUSALEM CROSS
CARYOPHYLLACEAE
There are several very different lychnis grown in our gardens, all thriving in full sun and well-drained soil. This is one of the best, with domes of bright red flowers on tall stems above deep green foliage, from mid- to late summer. Plant this perennial in the middle or at the back of the border.

LYCHNIS FLOS-CUCULI
RAGGED ROBIN
CARYOPHYLLACEAE
Ragged Robin, as its name suggests, has pink ragged flowers in early summer; these are used by bees for both pollen and nectar. Not common in the wild, it is worth encouraging in a damp corner of the garden. It is used as a food plant by butterflies. This perennial likes moist, moderately fertile soil.

Full-colour photograph to identify each plant

Symbols giving growth information at a glance

KEY TO THE SYMBOLS

EASY TO GROW

These are tolerant plants that require no special care or conditions in order to flourish.

MODERATE TO GROW

These are plants that require some special care, such as protection from frost.

DIFFICULT TO GROW

These are plants that require a great deal of specialized care, and offer a challenge for the more experienced gardener.

EVERGREEN

SEMI-EVERGREEN

DECIDUOUS

Deciduous plants lose all their leaves in autumn (sometimes in summer), while evergreen plants keep their foliage all year. Plants described as semi-evergreen may keep some or all of their foliage through the winter in sheltered gardens or if the weather is mild.

FEATURE LEAVES

FEATURE SCENT

FEATURE FLOWER

FEATURE FRUIT

These symbols indicate the main feature of interest for each plant in the directory, although this is not necessarily the plant's only attractive asset. Some plants are given more than one symbol. This information will help you to choose plants that have complementary features, or plants that will perform a specific function in your garden.

  RAPID GROWTH

MODERATE GROWTH

SLOW GROWTH

Speed of growth, like ease of growth, is a highly subjective category, and will vary according to local conditions. Rapid growth indicates plants that reach their full extent in a single season (annuals for instance), or plants that make substantial progress towards filling the space allowed for them in a single season. Slow growth indicates plants, such as trees and some shrubs, that take several seasons to reach their ultimate size. Moderate growth relates therefore to rates of progress between these two extremes.

SEASON OF INTEREST

The period of the year when a plant is likely to be most attractive is also indicated in a vertical bar to the right of each entry. Those plants that have something to offer all year round are marked accordingly. This will help you in creating a planting plan for each season.

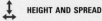 **HEIGHT AND SPREAD**

The size of plants will vary according to the growing conditions in your garden, so these measurements are a rough guide only. The measurements refer to the size of plants and trees when mature, although there are specific circumstances where the ultimate size is never reached.

 FULL SUN

PARTIAL SUN

SHADE

An indication of light preference is given to show each plant's optimum growing situation. Here again, this is only a rough guide, as some plants that prefer sun may also be reasonably tolerant of shade.

ANNUALS AND BIENNIALS

ALCEA ROSEA (SYN. ALTHEA ROSEA)
HOLLYHOCK
MALVACEAE

An old cottage garden plant also known as *Althea rosea* which is now best grown as an annual. Place at the back of the border where the tall spikes of crumpled silky blooms can be seen at their best. There are mixtures of colours available in either single or double blooms. Grow in well-drained, moderately fertile soil.

1.8m / 30cm

ANCHUSA CAPENSIS
SUMMER FORGET-ME-NOT
BORAGINACEAE

A biennial that is often grown as a hardy annual. The plants form compact mounds of deep blue flowers that appear throughout the summer. One of the best is 'Blue Angel', with marine-blue flowers. Mix with marigolds for a really colourful planting scheme. Grow in moist, well-drained, fertile soil.

20–45cm / 20cm

ANTIRRHINUM MAJUS
SNAPDRAGON
SCROPHULARIACEAE

Spikes of lipped flowers that 'snap' when squeezed, and are available in almost every colour except blue and purple. Always plant F1 hybrids, which are resistant to the disease rust; look for 'Liberty F1 mixed' for taller plants, or the dwarf 'Magic Carpet Mixed'. Grow in fertile, well-drained soil.

15–60cm / 20–30cm

BEGONIA SEMPERFLORENS
FIBROUS-ROOTED BEGONIA
BEGONIACEAE

One of the most popular bedding plants for sun or shade and suitable for beds, pots, hanging baskets or windowboxes. Can be grown from seed but is readily available as small plants in late spring. There are varieties with bronze rather than green leaves and the flower colours include white, pink, orange and red.

20–30cm / 30cm

BRACTEANTHA BRACTEATA
EVERLASTING FLOWERS
ASTERACEAE

An annual also known as *Helichrysum bracteatum* which produces extraordinary papery flowers in a range of colours which can be cut and dried. The easiest for children to grow are dwarf varieties like 'Bright Bikini' which form neat plants that do not need staking. It likes moderately fertile, well-drained soil.

30–90cm / 30cm

CALENDULA OFFICINALIS
MARIGOLD
ASTERACEAE

Children love these bright annuals which, unless dead-headed, will seed themselves all over the garden. The daisy-like flowers may be double or single, with a colour range from creamy yellow through lemon and gold to deep orange. The old-fashioned single orange form is still the best. Grow in well-drained soil.

30–60cm / 30cm

SPRING | SUMMER | AUTUMN | WINTER

leaf type   light preference   speed of growth   ease of growth

CENTAUREA CYANUS
CORNFLOWER
ASTERACEAE

Our native cornflower, with dark blue, thistle-like flowers on wiry stems. There are a range of cultivated varieties including white, pink and maroon flowers. The best variety for children to grow is the dwarf blue 'Blue Baby', which will stay neat and tidy whatever the weather. This annual likes well-drained soil.

20–80cm
20cm

CLARKIA AMOENA (SYN. GODETIA GRANDIFLORA)
GODETIA
ONAGRACEAE

Another easy annual for children to grow, with large papery flowers in July and August. Look for the smaller varieties like 'Salmon Princess' with pink flowers or 'Dwarf Satin' with assorted colours, as these will not need staking. They are good for any soil, including poor soils.

30–60cm
30cm

CLARKIA UNGUICULATA (SYN. CLARKIA ELEGANS)
ONAGRACEAE

A vigorous annual that bears spikes of ruffle-edged flowers that look like miniature hollyhocks. The flowers can be red, pink or mauve and occasionally white. Easy to grow as long as they are sown where they are to flower as they dislike being moved. It likes soil that is moderately fertile, well drained but moist, and if possible, slightly acid.

30–60cm
20cm

COSMOS BIPINNATUS
COSMEA
ASTERACEAE

A lovely annual for dry soils and full sun, with ferny leaves and flowers like a single dahlia. Older varieties have white or pink flowers, but there are newer cultivars with red, striped and even chocolate-coloured flowers. Plant in a group or among taller plants. Prefers well-drained, sandy soil.

45–95cm
30cm

DIANTHUS BARBATUS
SWEET WILLIAM
CARYOPHYLLACEAE

An annual or biennial with a wonderful scent that children love. The flat heads of massed flowers are available in white, pink and red, and in a range of types from tall varieties grown as biennials to the dwarf 'Wee Willie', which is only 15cm (6in) high and grown as an annual. It likes any well-drained soil.

15–60cm
30cm

ERIGERON 'KARVINSKIANUS'
SPANISH DAISY
ASTERACEAE

A spreading annual that is covered with pink-backed white daisies that turn pink and then almost purple as they age. They flower all summer long and are best planted as small plants and allowed plenty of room. An excellent choice for children's windowboxes and containers. It likes any well-drained soil.

30cm
50cm

⬍ height and spread   ✳ feature of interest   ▮▮▮▮ season of interest   *ANNUALS AND BIENNIALS A – E*

ANNUALS AND BIENNIALS

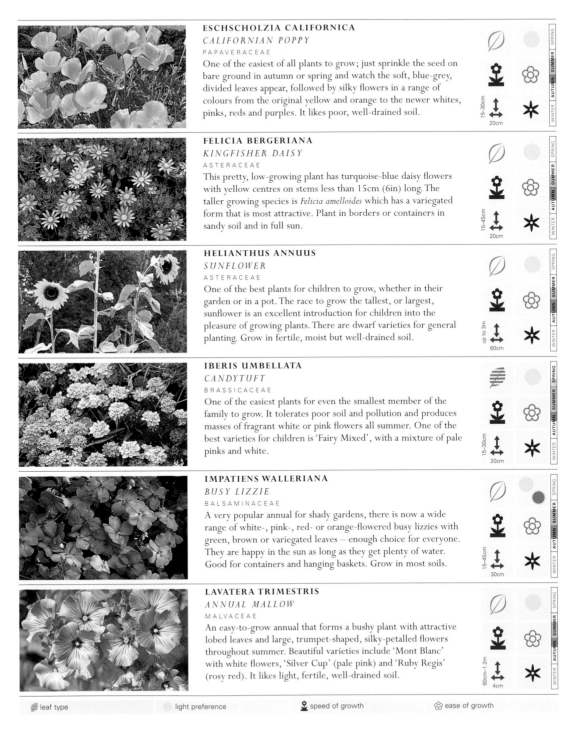

ESCHSCHOLZIA CALIFORNICA
CALIFORNIAN POPPY
PAPAVERACEAE

One of the easiest of all plants to grow; just sprinkle the seed on bare ground in autumn or spring and watch the soft, blue-grey, divided leaves appear, followed by silky flowers in a range of colours from the original yellow and orange to the newer whites, pinks, reds and purples. It likes poor, well-drained soil.

15–30cm
20cm

FELICIA BERGERIANA
KINGFISHER DAISY
ASTERACEAE

This pretty, low-growing plant has turquoise-blue daisy flowers with yellow centres on stems less than 15cm (6in) long. The taller growing species is *Felicia amelloides* which has a variegated form that is most attractive. Plant in borders or containers in sandy soil and in full sun.

15–45cm
20cm

HELIANTHUS ANNUUS
SUNFLOWER
ASTERACEAE

One of the best plants for children to grow, whether in their garden or in a pot. The race to grow the tallest, or largest, sunflower is an excellent introduction for children into the pleasure of growing plants. There are dwarf varieties for general planting. Grow in fertile, moist but well-drained soil.

up to 3m
60cm

IBERIS UMBELLATA
CANDYTUFT
BRASSICACEAE

One of the easiest plants for even the smallest member of the family to grow. It tolerates poor soil and pollution and produces masses of fragrant white or pink flowers all summer. One of the best varieties for children is 'Fairy Mixed', with a mixture of pale pinks and white.

15–30cm
20cm

IMPATIENS WALLERIANA
BUSY LIZZIE
BALSAMINACEAE

A very popular annual for shady gardens, there is now a wide range of white-, pink-, red- or orange-flowered busy lizzies with green, brown or variegated leaves – enough choice for everyone. They are happy in the sun as long as they get plenty of water. Good for containers and hanging baskets. Grow in most soils.

15–45cm
30cm

LAVATERA TRIMESTRIS
ANNUAL MALLOW
MALVACEAE

An easy-to-grow annual that forms a bushy plant with attractive lobed leaves and large, trumpet-shaped, silky-petalled flowers throughout summer. Beautiful varieties include 'Mont Blanc' with white flowers, 'Silver Cup' (pale pink) and 'Ruby Regis' (rosy red). It likes light, fertile, well-drained soil.

60cm–1.2m
4cm

leaf type   light preference   speed of growth   ease of growth

LIMNANTHES DOUGLASII
POACHED EGG PLANT
LIMANTHACEAE

The poached egg plant, as its name suggests, has flowers with white edges and golden yellow centres. Very easy to grow, there is the added bonus of pretty ferny leaves and a delicate scent. It tends to spread seed all over the garden, so be warned! Grow in fertile, moist but well-drained soil.

15cm
15cm

LOBELIA ERINUS
LOBELIA
CAMPANULACEAE

Used for generations as a bedding plant with alyssum and salvias, the blue-flowered lobelia is still as popular as ever. Use the dwarf forms like 'Crystal Palace' as edging, and the trailing ones like 'Sapphire' to cascade over the edges of hanging baskets. Water well in dry weather and grow in slightly moist soil.

20cm
15cm

LOBULARIA MARITIMA
SWEET ALYSSUM
BRASSICACEAE

This annual, also known as *Alyssum maritimum*, has been used for years as part of colourful bedding schemes. The leaves are covered with scented white flowers through summer. Easy to grow in all but very fertile soils, there are now newer varieties with lilac and purple flowers.

7-15cm
20cm

LUNARIA ANNUA
HONESTY
BRASSICACEAE

Produces loose clusters of scented purple or white flowers then disc-like pods that can be carefully split to unfold the silvery plate in the middle. This biennial is an important food plant for Orange Tip caterpillars. Sow seeds at the back of a border in moist but well-drained soil and allow plants to self-seed.

75cm
30cm

MATTHIOLA BICORNIS
NIGHT-SCENTED STOCK
BRASSICACEAE

This annual may be a mistake to give to children, as they may insist on staying up to smell the purple flowers which open to release their rich fragrance as the sun sets. It is so easy to grow that it is a must for the whole family. Grow in moist but well-drained, moderately fertile soil.

35cm
20cm

MYOSOTIS ALPESTRIS
FORGET-ME-NOT
BORAGINACEAE

Forget-me-nots growing among tulips are a must for spring. There are now pink and white varieties but the traditional blue is still the best, particularly the new dwarf 'Blue Ball'. These perennials, grown as biennials, freely self-seed and will appear year after year. Grow in moist but well-drained soil.

20cm
15cm

↕ height and spread   ✳ feature of interest   ▮▮▮ season of interest   *ANNUALS AND BIENNIALS* **E – M**

ANNUALS AND BIENNIALS

NEMOPHILA MENZIESII
CALIFORNIAN BLUEBELL
HYDROPHYLLACEAE

Low mounds of feathery leaves give rise to bright blue, buttercup-like flowers all summer long. Easy to grow in any fertile soil, they are a lovely annual for containers or mixed with *Limnanthes douglasii* in a children's garden. Keep them watered in dry weather. Grow in moist but well-drained, fertile soil.

NICOTIANA ALATA
TOBACCO PLANT
SOLANACEAE

Look for the hybrids of tobacco plant with white, pink or pale green flowers that usually, but not always, are scented in the evening. One of the prettiest is 'Havana Appleblossom' with white flowers and pink backs, or try 'Lime Green' with yellow-green blooms. Grow in any fertile, moist but well-drained soil.

NIGELLA DAMASCENA
LOVE-IN-A-MIST
RANUNCULACEAE

A favourite cottage annual that just needs seeds scattering on the bare ground in spring for a delightful display of feathery leaves and blue, spiky flowers in midsummer. Even more attractive, for most children, are the 'poppable' fruits that follow. There are varieties with pink and white flowers. It likes almost any soil.

OENOTHERA BIENNIS
EVENING PRIMROSE
ONAGRACEAE

As its name suggests, this plant opens its flowers and emits its fragrance in the evening, but the large, almost translucent, lemon-yellow flowers are worth the wait as they positively glow as the light fades. These biennials need to be sown in the autumn to flower the following summer. Grow in any well-drained soil.

PAPAVER NUDICAULE
ICELANDIC POPPY
PAPAVERACEAE

Poppies look delicate with their papery-thin petals and bowed heads, but are surprisingly tough and easy to grow. The Icelandic poppy can be treated as an annual and sown in spring to produce its white, yellow, orange or red flowers throughout the summer. A perennial grown as an annual, it likes fertile, well-drained soil.

PETUNIA X HYBRIDA
PETUNIA
SOLANACEAE

Petunias love hot, dry summers and suffer when the weather is wet and cold, but they are always worth growing. Showy, funnel-shaped flowers come in a range of colours. There are varieties that stay neat and compact for edging, and trailing varieties for hanging baskets. Grow in any well-drained soil.

leaf type — light preference — speed of growth — ease of growth

PHACELIA TANACETIFOLIA
CALIFORNIAN BLUEBELL
HYDROPHYLLACEAE

An annual well known to beekeepers as it secretes nectar very freely and is visited by bees throughout the day. Easy to grow from seed, it has greyish foliage and large, bell-shaped flowers of mauvish blue. It succeeds in most well-drained soils and in both sun and partial shade.

60cm · 20cm

RESEDA ODORATA
MIGNONETTE
RESEDACEAE

Mignonette is another old favourite much prized for its intense, spicy fragrance. The greenish-yellow flowers of this annual appear in odd cone-like trusses in mid- to late summer. Look for a variety like 'Sweet Scented' or 'Fragrant Beauty' for maximum scent, and grow in well-drained, fertile, slightly alkaline soil.

30–60cm · 30cm

SALVIA SPLENDENS
RED SAGE
LAMIACEAE

The traditional red, spike-like, bedding salvia has undergone a transformation and is now available in a wonderful range of colours, including salmon, purple, plum, pink and white. However, the bright-red-flowered 'Vanguard' is still the most popular. Grow in moist but well-drained soil.

30–45cm · 20cm

SCABIOSA ATROPURPUREA
SWEET SCABIOUS
DIPSACACEAE

The large round flower heads of this annual come in a range of colours including white, blue, pink, lilac and red. Some of the varieties are tall and need staking so look for the smaller plants like 'Dwarf Double Mixed'. It is easy to grow except in a really wet summer. It likes most soils.

60–75cm · 30cm

TAGETES PATULA
FRENCH MARIGOLD
ASTERACEAE

Compact plants with deeply divided foliage and small orange and yellow flowers like miniature dahlias. Good varieties include 'Naughty Marietta', with single golden flowers with a maroon centre, and 'Juliette', with double flowers of yellow striped with terracotta. Grow in moderately fertile, well-drained soil.

30cm · 20cm

VIOLA X WITTROCKIANA
PANSY
VIOLACEAE

Pansies are now available for flowering throughout the year. Almost every flower colour is available except green. Choose 'Universal' pansies for winter and spring flowers, and 'Turbo' for pansies in summer; for really large flowers there is 'Mammoth Giant'. Grow in moist but well-drained, humus-rich soil.

20cm · 30cm

---

‡ height and spread   ✳ feature of interest   ▭ season of interest   *ANNUALS AND BIENNIALS* **N – V**

BULBS

CROCUS X LUTEUS
CROCUS
IRIDACEAE

There are lots of different crocus species to grow, including those that flower in the autumn as well as the better-known winter and early spring flowers. This is the large Dutch crocus, with yellow, white or purple flowers in early spring which is ideally suited to planting in grass. Grow in any well-drained soil.

ERANTHIS HYEMALIS
WINTER ACONITE
RANUNCULACEAE

Winter aconites, together with snowdrops, are the earliest of the bulbs to flower; their glossy yellow flowers appear in January or early February. Plant in the grass, or under trees and shrubs in fertile, humus-rich soil, to form a golden carpet, or, in a small garden, plant a small patch by the back door.

GALANTHUS NIVALIS
SNOWDROP
AMARYLLIDACEAE

Snowdrops are the popular heralds of spring, with their nodding white and green flowers and dark green leaves. There are several different species and cultivars, with double flowers such as 'Flore Pleno'. Dried-out bulbs are not successful, so plant as soon as you get them. Grow in moist but well-drained soil.

HYACINTHOIDES NON-SCRIPTA
BLUEBELL
HYACINTHACEAE

Not a perennial for the small garden as you really need an area of woodland to grow bluebells successfully, but even a small grove of birch trees can be transformed with a carpet of bluebells in the spring. Plant in autumn as soon as possible after purchase. It likes moderately fertile, moist but well-drained soil.

HYACINTHUS ORIENTALIS
HYACINTH
HYACINTHACEAE

Hyacinths produce large trusses of scented flowers in spring, and are ideal for planting in containers or borders for a bright patch of colour. The colour range includes the traditional blue, pink and white flowers but also plum, apricot and pale yellow. Grow in well-drained, moderately fertile soil.

IRIS RETICULATA
DWARF IRIS
IRIDACEAE

There are dozens of different irises we can use in our gardens, but this is one of the smallest, earliest and prettiest, with thin grey-green leaves and deep purple, sweetly scented flowers in early spring. Grow at the front of a bed or in pots near the house in moderately fertile, well-drained soil.

| leaf type | light preference | speed of growth | ease of growth |

LILIUM REGALE
REGAL LILY
LILIACEAE

If you grow just one lily it should be this one, with tall stems of large, white, trumpet-like flowers with pink stripes on the back of the petals, a yellow throat and a wonderfully rich scent. The easiest way to grow lilies is in pots using organically rich compost, or well-drained, fertile soil.

1–1.5m / 30cm

MUSCARI ARMENIACUM
GRAPE HYACINTH
HYACINTHACEAE

The flowers, which appear in spring, resemble miniature blue hyacinths and look wonderful planted with pink, white or yellow tulips at the front of a border. Very easy to grow, it can also be used as ground cover under shrubs and will spread quite happily if left to itself. It likes moist but well-drained soil.

20cm / 5cm

NARCISSUS POETICUS
POET'S EYE NARCISSUS
AMARYLLIDACEAE

This narcissus has white petals and a small, frilled, red-edged cup. Very sweetly scented, they are almost the last of the narcissus to flower, and for that reason can be a problem grown in grass as the grass will need cutting before the leaves have died down. It is best grown in borders or containers. Grow in any soil.

30–45cm / 20cm

NARCISSUS PSEUDONARCISSUS
DAFFODIL
AMARYLLIDACEAE

This is the most popular flower in our gardens, and a familiar sight planted in grass in the spring. Use the simpler, yellow-flowered varieties for planting in grass areas and keep the doubles, multi-colours and frilly petalled cultivars to grow in beds, borders and containers. Grow in any soil.

10–50cm / 20cm

SCILLA SIBERICA
SCILLA
HYACINTHACEAE

Looking like small bluebells, scillas are very easy plants to grow. Once planted, they will happily spread through the rockery, or as a carpet under trees and shrubs. Plant the bulbs immediately after purchase as they are susceptible to decay when out of the soil. Grow in well-drained, moderately fertile soil.

10cm / 5cm

TULIPA HYBRIDS
TULIP
LILIACEAE

Unsurpassed in their range of colours, tulips are also available in different heights and with different times of flowering, the earliest species being in flower with crocuses and the latest tulip hybrids flowering almost with the early roses. They are suitable for beds, borders and containers. Grow in any soil.

up to 75cm / 20cm

↕ height and spread   ✳ feature of interest   ▮▮▮▮ season of interest   *BULBS C – T*

HERBACEOUS PERENNIALS

ACANTHUS MOLLIS
BEAR'S BREECHES
ACANTHACEAE

A wonderful architectural perennial with large, shiny, dark green leaves and tall spikes of mauve and white flowers in late summer. It is most effective planted in the corner of a bed or border where it catches the eye, or grown in a large container placed against a wall. Grow in any well-drained soil.

1.2m / 60cm

ACHILLEA MILLEFOLIUM
YARROW
ASTERACEAE

An old-fashioned herbaceous perennial with grey-green ferny foliage and flat heads of tiny flowers in a wide variety of colours. Very easy to grow – the white-flowered form is often found as a weed of our lawns. Flowering from early summer through into the autumn, they love sun and well-drained soil.

90cm / 60cm

ALCHEMILLA MOLLIS
LADY'S MANTLE
ROSACEAE

One of the plants for every garden, this will grow practically anywhere and flowers almost continuously all summer. The soft-green rounded leaves collect water around their edge like a string of jewels and the tiny greenish-yellow flowers are carried in foamy clusters. Grow in any well-drained soil.

60cm / 75cm

ANEMONE HUPEHENSIS
JAPANESE ANEMONE
RANUNCULACEAE

An elegant perennial plant with clusters of pink or white, cup-shaped, single, double or semi-double flowers, borne on upright stems for long periods in late summer. Long-lived, vigorous and easy to grow, it makes a great back-of-the-border plant. Grow in moist, fertile soil. This plant is mildly poisonous.

60cm–1.2m / 60cm

AQUILEGIA VULGARIS
COLUMBINE
RANUNCULACEAE

A delightful flowering perennial and a favourite with children, columbine has grey-green, fern-like leaves and extraordinary flowers which come in a wide variety of colours, and many are bi-coloured. Very easy to grow in any soil, it will happily seed itself all over the garden if you want it to. It is mildly poisonous.

60–90cm / 45cm

ASTER SPP.
PERENNIAL DAISY
ASTERACEAE

Perennial daisies are easy to grow, but many varieties tend to have short flowering periods, be susceptible to mildew and require staking. Choose a cultivar like *Aster amellus* 'Violet Queen', a trouble-free dwarf variety with a profusion of violet flowers that are attractive to butterflies. It likes any soil.

60cm–1.2m / 45–60cm

SPRING | SUMMER | AUTUMN | WINTER

≣ leaf type   ● light preference   ♣ speed of growth   ⚘ ease of growth

ASTRANTIA MAJOR
MASTERWORT
APIACEAE

A showy, easy-to-grow perennial that forms neat mounds of palmate leaves and erect stems of starry domes of pinky-white flowers in early summer. There are very attractive cultivars with dark crimson flowers and others with variegated leaves. It is good in borders or as ground cover. Grow in any well-drained soil.

60cm / 45cm

AUBRIETA DELTOIDEA
AUBRETIA
BRASSICACEAE

A low-growing perennial that is often planted on top of low walls so that the flowers form a mauve or purple 'cascade' in the spring. Good for a sunny position, cut back after flowering. It is a favourite of the Small Tortoiseshell and Wall Brown butterflies. Grow in moderately fertile, neutral to alkaline, well-drained soil.

10cm / 60cm

BELLIS PERENNIS
DAISY
ASTERACEAE

Daisies hardly need planting, as they tend to pop up as weeds in our flowerbeds and lawns. Encourage their growth in longer grass areas to allow enough flowers for making daisy chains. Alternatively plant some of the double varieties like 'Robella' in the front of children's beds and borders. Grow in any soil.

15cm / 20cm

BERGENIA CORDIFOLIA
ELEPHANT'S EARS
SAXIFRAGACEAE

A handsome evergreen plant with large, rounded, shiny green leaves that sometimes turn bright red in winter. Thick, fleshy flower stems hold up clusters of hanging pink flowers. An excellent edging or ground-cover plant, it grows almost anywhere but is best in light shade and rich soil.

45cm / 60cm

BUTOMUS UMBELLATUS
FLOWERING RUSH
BUTOMACEAE

Flowering rush is a lovely marginal plant with bright pink, almond-scented flowers in late summer rising above rush-like leaves. The leaves are very sharp, so place within the pond and grow other plants in front for protection. A range of insects visit for nectar. Grow in rich mud or in water to 25cm (10in) deep.

1.5m / 45cm

CALTHA PALUSTRIS
MARSH MARIGOLD
RANUNCULACEAE

This is the first of the water plants to flower, producing a mass of bright yellow buttercup flowers in the early spring. It will grow in the water or in wet or just damp soil around the pond. There are double and white-flowered cultivars, but the native single yellow is much the prettiest.

30-40cm / 45cm

↕ height and spread   ✳ feature of interest   ▭▭▭ season of interest   *HERBACEOUS PERENNIALS **A – C***

HERBACEOUS PERENNIALS

CAMPANULA GLOMERATA
BELLFLOWER
CAMPANULACEAE

There are lots of bellflowers, from prostrate ones that will grow in gaps in paving to tall stately flowers for the back of the border. This middle-of-the-border plant has rounded heads of deep-purple flowers. Easy to grow in almost any moist but well-drained soil.

60cm / 45cm

CAMPANULA ROTUNDIFOLIA
HAREBELL
CAMPANULACEAE

With their dainty, nodding, blue flowers and slender stems, these perennials are easy to grow in almost any conditions. Sow seed in windowboxes, containers, beds and borders, or add some plants to a wild flower meadow. Bees visit the flowers for pollen and nectar. Grow in moist but well-drained soil.

15–40cm / 30cm

CARDAMINE PRATENSIS
LADY'S SMOCK
BRASSICACEAE

A lovely native herbaceous perennial that likes to grow in damp grassland but is just as happy in the moist soil around a pond. Plant with ragged robin for a pretty spring display. Easily grown from seed sown where it is to grow, it is the food plant for Orange Tip and Brown caterpillars.

15–40cm / 30cm

CENTRANTHUS RUBER
RED VALERIAN
VALERIANACEAE

The deep red flower heads and grey-green leaves of red valerian are frequently seen growing in rocky crevices and gaps in paving, but it can be grown in any well-drained soil which is not too rich. It is a favourite source of nectar for some of our prettiest butterflies, including Small Tortoiseshells.

30–90cm / 30cm

CERASTIUM TOMENTOSUM
SNOW-IN-SUMMER
CARYOPHYLLACEAE

A carpet of snowy white flowers above a bed of grey leaves describes this perennial, one of the very easiest of all plants to grow. Seen at its best covering banks or hanging over low walls, it is so vigorous that it has a habit of covering large areas of the garden, whether wanted or not. Grow in any soil.

15cm / 60cm

COREOPSIS VERTICILLATA
TICKSEED
ASTERACEAE

Low-growing domes of fine, narrow, dark-green leaves give rise to masses of yellow daisy-like flowers from midsummer right through to the autumn. Choose a named variety like 'Moonbeam', with pale yellow flowers, and plant it at the front of the border in fertile, well-drained soil.

80cm / 45cm

SPRING | SUMMER | AUTUMN | WINTER

| leaf type | light preference | speed of growth | ease of growth |

DICENTRA SPECTABILIS
BLEEDING HEART
PAPAVERACEAE

A plant with graceful, deeply divided, grey-green leaves and strange, heart-shaped, bright pink flowers with a white point that hangs down from the arching flower stems. There is also an equally attractive all-white-flowered variety. Good for shady areas of the garden and moist, fertile soil. It is mildly poisonous.

50cm
45cm

ECHINOPS RITRO
GLOBE THISTLE
ASTERACEAE

A statuesque perennial plant for the back of the border, with grey-green, deeply divided leaves and large, round, spiky blue flower heads in midsummer. It requires little attention, apart from cutting back in the autumn. The flowers are visited by both bees and butterflies. Grow in any well-drained soil.

60cm–1.5m
60cm

ERIGERON SPECIOSUS
FLEABANE
ASTERACEAE

These plants look like dwarf Michaelmas daisies except that they flower in mid- rather than late summer. An easily grown plant for the front of the border, it has masses of purple or lilac daisy flowers with bright yellow centres. The flowers are visited by both bees and butterflies. Grow in fertile, well-drained soil.

60cm
45cm

EUPATORIUM CANNABINUM
HEMP AGRIMONY
ASTERACEAE

A bold perennial for damp soil at the water's edge, the tall flower stems are topped with domes of pink flowers throughout the summer. Fluffy seeds form after the flowers but these should be cut off to prevent seeds spreading all over the garden. The flowers are visited by bees and butterflies.

1.2m
60cm

FILIPENDULA ULMARIA
MEADOWSWEET
ROSACEAE

Also known as Queen-of-the-Meadows, this is an elegant plant producing tall stems of sweetly scented, fluffy cream flowers above fern-like foliage. There are variegated and golden-leaved cultivars that look lovely in ornamental bog gardens. Bees use the flowers for pollen. Grow in leafy, moist soil.

60cm–1.2m
60cm

GERANIUM X OXONIANUM 'WARGRAVE PINK'
CRANE'S BILL
GERANIACEAE

The herbaceous geraniums are among the best and most useful of all garden plants. If you have never grown these plants, then 'Wargrave Pink' is probably the best one with which to start, having semi-evergreen, bright green leaves and salmon-pink flowers for most of the summer. It will do well in most soils.

45cm
45cm

⬍ height and spread　　　✳ feature of interest　　　▨ season of interest　　　*HERBACEOUS PERENNIALS* **C – G**

HERBACEOUS PERENNIALS

GEUM 'BORISII'
AVENS
ROSACEAE

There are not many garden plants with orange flowers, and this is one of the best and the easiest to grow. With attractive domes of bright green, lobed and indented leaves and round, bright orange flowers from late spring to midsummer, this is good for the front of the border. Grow in fertile, well-drained soil.

45cm / 45cm

HEMEROCALLIS HYBRIDS
DAY LILY
HEMEROCALLIDACEAE

Handsome, robust and trouble-free plants that belong in every garden as they grow in almost any soil from dry ground to standing in water. The lily-like flowers last only a day, but there are always plenty of replacement buds. Varieties are available in a range of sizes and colours.

80cm / 60cm

HESPERIS MATRONALIS
SWEET ROCKET
BRASSICACEAE

A short-lived perennial that is frequently grown as a biennial. The pretty white or violet flowers become fragrant in the late afternoon and evening. The leaves are a food plant for Orange Tip caterpillars and the flowers are visited by butterflies for nectar. Grow in fertile, moist soil.

40-90cm / 45cm

HEUCHERA SANGUINEA
CORAL FLOWER
SAXIFRAGACEAE

Long-lived evergreen plants for edging beds and borders whether in sun or light shade. Round, glossy green leaves form neat domes of foliage from which rise thin wiry stems of clustered tiny pink or red flowers in late spring or early summer. Grow in moist but well-drained, fertile soil.

45cm / 45cm

IRIS PSEUDACORUS
YELLOW FLAG
IRIDACEAE

Our native water iris grows in the water, in wet soil and in damp borders. It is a stately plant, with sword-like leaves and yellow flowers in midsummer. When grown in water, dragonfly larvae pupate on the leaves. Grow in the margins of a pond or any other wet place.

40cm-1.5m / 60cm

LEUCANTHEMUM X SUPERBUM
SHASTA DAISY
ASTERACEAE

Shasta daisies are so tough that they survive total neglect, and can be found growing in gardens that have been left untouched for several years. Large white daisies arise from somewhat coarse dark green leaves throughout the summer. 'Esther Read' is a good double-flowered form. Grow in any soil.

90cm / 60cm

≣ leaf type   ● light preference   ⚘ speed of growth   ⚙ ease of growth

LEUCANTHEMUM VULGARE
OX-EYE DAISY
ASTERACEAE

These large white and yellow perennials are one of the easiest wild flowers to grow, and they flower throughout the summer months. They can be planted in long grass as part of a wild flower meadow or as part of a planted bed or border. Easy to grow from seed sown where the plants are to flower. Grow in any soil.

20-80cm
45cm

LINARIA VULGARIS
TOADFLAX
SCROPHULARIACEAE

Also called butter and eggs, the flowers of this plant resemble small yellow snapdragons and hold a fascination for small children. It can be grown from seed and is best grown in grass areas or the wild garden. An important nectar plant for many bees. Grow in moderately fertile, light, sandy soil.

30-60cm
30cm

LIRIOPE MUSCARI
LILY TURF
CONVALLARIACEAE

A less frequently seen perennial with dark green, strap-like, arching leaves and low spikes of purple flowers in late summer right through the autumn. Easy to grow in sun or shade, the foliage is evergreen and it makes a good edging plant or ground cover beneath shrubs. Grow in well-drained soil.

40cm
45cm

LOTUS CORNICULATUS
BIRD'S FOOT TREFOIL
PAPILIONACEAE

A little herbaceous perennial that is found throughout the British Isles and produces a cluster of bright yellow pea flowers, succeeded by black pods that look like a claw or 'bird's foot'. Easy to grow from seed, it is an important food plant for the larvae of several butterflies. It likes any well-drained soil.

30cm
30cm

LYCHNIS CHALCEDONICA
JERUSALEM CROSS
CARYOPHYLLACEAE

There are several very different lychnis grown in our gardens, all thriving in full sun and well-drained soil. This is one of the best, with domes of bright red flowers on tall stems above deep green foliage, from mid- to late summer. Plant this perennial in the middle or at the back of the border.

90cm
45cm

LYCHNIS FLOS-CUCULI
RAGGED ROBIN
CARYOPHYLLACEAE

Ragged Robin, as its name suggests, has pink ragged flowers in early summer; these are used by bees for both pollen and nectar. Not common in the wild, it is worth encouraging in a damp corner of the garden. It is used as a food plant by butterflies. This perennial likes moist, moderately fertile soil.

30-60cm
45cm

⬍ height and spread   ✳ feature of interest   ▮▮▮ season of interest   *HERBACEOUS PERENNIALS* **G – L**

HERBACEOUS PERENNIALS

LYSIMACHIA VULGARIS
YELLOW LOOSESTRIFE
PRIMULACEAE

A tall, handsome perennial with spikes of bright yellow flowers, yellow loosestrife is very easy to grow, requiring no attention once planted. A native of our river banks, it prefers fertile soils with plenty of moisture but seems to thrive in almost any conditions.

60cm–1.2m / 60cm

LYTHRUM SALICARIA
PURPLE LOOSESTRIFE
LYTHRACEAE

A must for almost every garden, purple loosestrife will grow in water, or in wet or merely damp soil. Tall spires of brilliant reddish-purple flowers are produced from June to August and look wonderful growing with meadowsweet and water iris. An excellent plant for both bees and butterflies.

60cm–1.2m / 45cm

MENTHA AQUATICA
WATER MINT
LAMIACEAE

Like all mints, water mint can become invasive so it is best grown in a container placed in the pond or water's edge. The soft leaves are strongly aromatic, and the fluffy lilac-pink flowers are usually covered in butterflies and bees seeking nectar. Grow in a soil that is poor and moist.

90cm / 60cm

MYOSOTIS SCORPIOIDES
MARSH FORGET-ME-NOT
BORAGINACEAE

A perennial, aquatic version of the popular bedding forget-me-not, in which the leaves are smooth green and the heads of the blue flowers taller and less compact. An ideal plant for the edge of the pond. Butterflies visit the flowers for nectar. Grow in moderately fertile, moist or wet soil.

45cm / 45cm

NEPETA X FAASSENII
CATMINT
LAMIACEAE

Called catmint because cats love its spicy smell and will not only eat it but roll in it and curl up to sleep in the leaves, this is a very easy-to-grow plant that makes a lovely edge to a sunny border with grey-green leaves and lilac-blue flowers. During a hot sunny day the whole plant can be covered in bees. Grow in any soil.

45cm / 45cm

OENOTHERA TETRAGONA 'FIREWORKS'
SUNDROPS
ONAGRACEAE

A cheerful perennial plant for the front or middle of the border, with bronzy leaves and red, pointed buds on deep red stems that open to large, bright yellow, saucer-like flowers. They are easy to grow as long as they have a really sunny position and well-drained, fertile soil.

45cm / 45cm

≣ leaf type   ● light preference   ☘ speed of growth   ❀ ease of growth

ORIGANUM LAEVIGATUM 'HERRENHAUSEN'
MARJORAM
LAMIACEAE

One of the more ornamental forms of the herb marjoram, with aromatic leaves and tall stems of purple flowers throughout the late summer and autumn. All marjorams attract a wide range of butterflies, including Gatekeepers and Wall Browns. Grow in moderate, well-drained soil.

PENSTEMON BARBATUS
BEARDLIP PENSTEMON
SCROPHULARIACEAE

These perennials are some of the loveliest and most floriferous of our garden plants, with spikes of funnel-shaped flowers from midsummer to the first frosts. The green foliage is semi-evergreen. Select one of the tougher cultivars like 'Garnet' with deep red flowers. Grow in any well-drained soil.

PERSICARIA BISTORTA
BISTORT
POLYGONACEAE

A native plant that makes an attractive addition to the border, with its fresh green leaves and upright spikes of pink flowers in summer that look like miniature pokers. Very easy to grow; it looks after itself, just needing cutting back in winter. Birds, particularly finches, eat the seeds. Grow in any moist soil.

PHLOX PANICULATA
PERENNIAL PHLOX
POLEMONIACEAE

An almost essential perennial plant for the late summer border, with its tall domes of pink, white or lavender flowers held above rather dull green leaves. Some of the cultivars, particularly those with white flowers, are sweetly scented. It is easily grown in any well-fertilized, moist soil.

POLEMONIUM CAERULEUM
JACOB'S LADDER
POLEMONIACEAE

The neat, ladder-like arrangement of leaves gives this plant its common name. The upright flower stems carry clusters of purple-blue flowers in early summer. There are white flowered and variegated-leaved cultivars available. An easy plant for the border, it is happy in any well-drained soil.

PRIMULA X POLYANTHA
POLYANTHUS
PRIMULACEAE

Often grown as spring bedding plants, polyanthus also make good border plants where spring colour is needed. Available in a very wide range of colours, they prefer a moisture-retentive soil. If planting in a permanent position make sure you get a fully winter hardy variety as some cultivars are for growing indoors.

HERBACEOUS PERENNIALS

PRIMULA VERIS
COWSLIP
PRIMULACEAE

These nodding heads of yellow flowers rising out of a rosette of crumpled-looking leaves are an all-time favourite. When open, the flowers are sweetly scented. These perennials can be grown from seed in most garden soils or planted out as plants into a wild flower meadow.

20cm / 20cm

PRIMULA VULGARIS
PRIMROSE
PRIMULACEAE

In the wild, primroses grow on banks and below hedges, so try to find a shady slope in the garden and mix them with violets for an early spring display. You need plenty, as small children love to pick bunches as presents. You can also plant cultivated primroses which now come in a wide range of colours. It likes damp soils.

20cm / 35cm

SAGITTARIA SAGITTIFOLIA
ARROWHEAD
ALISMATACEAE

It is easy to see why this plant gets its name when clumps of large arrowhead-shaped leaves appear in the spring. Equally attractive are the spikes of white flowers with black centres. Plant at the water's edge so that the roots are covered in water. Prefers a fertile soil.

30-90cm / 60cm

SALVIA SUPERBA
PERENNIAL SAGE
LAMIACEAE

An indispensable plant for its spikes of small, tubular, deep purple flowers that bloom continuously the whole summer long. The attractive, grey-green leaves are, like most of the sages, aromatic. It is happy in any soil as long as it is well drained.

60-90cm / 45cm

SEDUM SPECTABILE
ICE PLANT
CRASSULACEAE

An easily grown perennial with grey-green fleshy leaves and flat domes of pink flowers in late summer and autumn that attract every butterfly within miles, including Red Admirals, Small Copper, Small Tortoiseshell and Speckled Wood. It is good for the front of a sunny border or grown in a pot. It likes most soils.

45cm / 45cm

SILENE DIOICA
RED CAMPION
CARYOPHYLLACEAE

Red campion has, in fact, pink flowers and, with primroses and violets, is found growing in banks and along hedgerows. Plant these three together in a shady corner of the garden for a pink, yellow and purple springtime display. It is also an important food plant for several moths. This perennial will grow in most soils.

45cm / 45cm

≣ leaf type	● light preference	⚓ speed of growth	✿ ease of growth

SOLIDAGO CANADENSIS
GOLDEN ROD
ASTERACEAE

A tough, easily grown plant with spikes of yellow flowers in late summer. The old taller golden rods were rather dull but there are new dwarf varieties like 'Golden Thumb' which is only 30cm (1ft) high and a good front-of-border plant. The flowers are visited by bees and butterflies. Grow in sandy, well-drained soil.

80cm–1.5m / 45–60cm

TRADESCANTIA X ANDERSONIANA
SPIDERWORT
COMMELINACEAE

An old cottage garden plant with tall, arching, strap-like foliage and odd three-cornered blue, purple or white flowers that nestle in the leaves and give it another name, 'Moses in the bulrushes'. Easy to grow in any soil, they flower right through the summer.

60cm / 60cm

VERONICA BECCABUNGA
BROOKLIME
SCROPHULARIACEAE

A pretty, low-growing plant that grows in shallow water or wet soil. The bright blue flowers appear throughout the summer and are attractive to honey bees. Sow seeds in wet soil or plant rooted stems. It looks most attractive as ground cover beneath taller waterside plants.

20–30cm

VERONICA SPICATA
SPIKED SPEEDWELL
SCROPHULARIACEAE

A plant with clumps of shiny green leaves and tall spikes of bright blue flowers, it is easy to grow given a sunny spot and well-drained soil. There are several cultivars, including the subspecies *incana*, with silvery-grey leaves. Like most of the veronicas, it is an excellent bee plant.

60cm / 45cm

VIOLA RIVINIANA
VIOLET
VIOLACEAE

The true violets of our hedgerows are not often seen in garden centres but they are well worth finding for children to grow. Once planted they quickly form a carpet of bright green leaves and deep violet flowers. These perennials are a major food plant for the larvae of several fritillary butterflies. They like most soils.

20cm / 40cm

VIOLA TRICOLOR
WILD PANSY
VIOLACEAE

Also known as Heartsease, this is a lovely plant for children producing flowers with pansy 'faces' from spring through to autumn. The flowers are usually purple and yellow, but vary in colour when grown from seed. Very easy to grow, it is best to treat as an annual and sow new seed every year. It likes any soil.

10–20cm / 30cm

SHRUBS

BUDDLEJA DAVIDII
BUTTERFLY BUSH
BUDDLEJACEAE

If you have room for only one shrub, *Buddleja* would be a good choice. It is very easy to grow, grows quickly, has long, furry leaves and large cones of white, lilac or deep purple flowers that are smothered in many of our loveliest butterflies throughout the late summer. Grow in well-drained soil.

3m
3m

CARYOPTERIS X CLANDONENSIS
BLUE SPIRAEA
VERBENACEAE

An excellent aromatic, grey-leaved shrub, with fluffy blue flowers in late summer. It needs a warm, sunny position and prefers chalky, well-drained soils. In a cold winter, the top growth may be killed off but new shoots will grow from the ground next spring. It is visited by both bees and butterflies.

1m
1.5m

CHOISYA TERNATA
MEXICAN ORANGE BLOSSOM
RUTACEAE

An evergreen shrub with bright green, aromatic leaves and clusters of white, scented flowers in late spring, often repeating intermittently throughout the summer. Very neat, it can be pruned to keep within a restricted space. Its only problem is that the leaves can be damaged by a cold winter. Grow in any soil.

2m
2m

CORNUS ALBA 'SPAETHII'
YELLOW-LEAVED DOGWOOD
CORNACEAE

Grown for its red winter stems and for its green and yellow foliage, this is a shrub with year-round interest that is easy to grow in almost any conditions including wet soils. For winter colour the stems should be cut back to the ground in the spring every few years. Grow in any soil.

2m
2m

CORYLUS AVELLANA
HAZEL
BETULACEAE

The hazel produces yellow catkins in early spring and is home to over 70 insect species which, in turn, are food for several birds. The cobnuts produced in autumn are food for squirrels and birds as well as humans! There are golden-leaved and even contorted garden forms. Grow in well-drained, fertile soil.

6m
6m

COTINUS COGGYGRIA 'ROYAL PURPLE'
PURPLE-SMOKE BUSH
ANACARDIACEAE

If you have room for a single, large, purple-leaved shrub, this is it. Fast growing, it quickly forms a round-topped spreading shrub with deep plum leaves that redden in the autumn and plumes of tiny purple-pink flowers. It is happy in almost any conditions but best in sun. It thrives in most soils.

5m
5m

leaf type   light preference   speed of growth   ease of growth

COTONEASTER FRIGIDUS 'CORNUBIA'
COTONEASTER
ROSACEAE

There are a great many different cotoneasters, almost all of which have orange and red berries in autumn that are popular with birds like thrushes and robins. This is one of the taller evergreen cotoneasters, with small white flowers and clusters of crimson-red fruits. Grow in well-drained, fertile soil.

5m

COTONEASTER HORIZONTALIS
HERRINGBONE COTONEASTER
ROSACEAE

This plant has low, arching branches on which the small leaves are arranged in a neat herringbone fashion. In summer, the plant is covered by small white flowers that bees visit constantly for nectar, followed by red berries which are frequently eaten by birds. Grow in any well-drained soil.

75cm / 1.5m

CYTISUS SCOPARIUS
BROOM
PAPILIONACEAE

An important plant for pollen collection by bees in late spring. Broom is a wild plant of heathland but there are a range of garden cultivars including 'Andreanus', which has bi-coloured crimson and yellow flowers, and 'Cornish Cream' with yellow and cream flowers. It likes slightly acid, well-drained soil.

2m / 2m

DEUTZIA SCABRA 'PLENA'
DEUTZIA
HYDRANGEAECEAE

A free-flowering shrub with olive-green leaves and clusters of double pinky-white flowers in late spring to early summer. Good in mixed borders, it is happy in most conditions but prefers sunny sites and plenty of moisture.

3m / 2m

ELAEAGNUS X EBBINGEI
ELAEAGNUS
ELAEAGNACEAE

A very useful, fast-growing evergreen that makes a good hedge or background shrub for the border. The grey-green leaves hide tiny sulphur-yellow flowers which appear in late summer and are very strongly and deliciously scented. There are forms available with variegated leaves. This plant enjoys fertile, well-drained soil.

3m / 3m

FORSYTHIA X INTERMEDIA 'LYNWOOD'
GOLDEN BELLS
OLEACEAE

A very popular shrub, partly because it is so easy to grow whatever the soil conditions, but mostly for its bright yellow, bell-shaped flowers in early spring that cover the branches before the leaves appear. Plant in a corner behind a patch of daffodils for a splash of spring colour.

3m / 3m

↕ height and spread   ✳ feature of interest   ▭ season of interest   *SHRUBS B – F*

SHRUBS

FUCHSIA 'RICCARTONII'
FUCHSIA
ONAGRACEAE

A firm favourite with children, who love popping the fat buds and making 'ballerinas' from the open flowers. A hardy fuchsia, with scarlet and violet flowers through the late summer and autumn. 'Mrs Popple' has slightly larger, rather more 'poppable' buds. Grow in fertile, well-drained soil.

1.2m · 1.5m

HEBE 'AUTUMN GLORY'
SHRUBBY VERONICA
SCROPHULARIACEAE

One of the best shrubs for all but the very coldest gardens. It forms neat rounded bushes with evergreen, purplish-green leaves and rounded clusters of deep purple flowers throughout the summer. All hebes are attractive to bees and many butterflies. Grow in poor to moderate, moist but well-drained soil.

60cm · 90cm

MAHONIA AQUIFOLIUM
OREGON GRAPE
BERBERIDACEAE

A useful evergreen shrub with dark green, holly-like leaves that turn purple-red in autumn, and bright yellow flowers in early spring. It spreads easily to form a carpet beneath other trees and shrubs. In autumn, blue-black berries are produced. Grow in soil that is moderately fertile, moist but well-drained.

1m · 1.5m

PEROVSKIA ATRIPLICIFOLIA
RUSSIAN SAGE
LAMIACEAE

A sun-loving shrub with grey-green, aromatic, deeply divided leaves, and spikes of lavender-blue in late summer. May suffer in a cold winter but will produce new shoots from the base. Plant in well-drained soil in the middle or back of the border. Popular with bees gathering nectar.

1.5m · 60cm

PHILADELPHUS 'BELLE ETOILE'
MOCK ORANGE
HYDRANGEACEAE

Mock oranges are unequalled for summer scent, a single bush being capable of scenting the whole of a small garden. 'Belle Etoile' is one of the best to grow, being a medium-sized shrub with white, single flowers with a maroon blotch and a wonderful fragrance. Grow in any moderately fertile, well-drained soil.

1.5m · 2m

POTENTILLA FRUTICOSA
SHRUBBY CINQUEFOIL
ROSACEAE

This is a low, rounded shrub with tiny leaves and a mass of small, single, saucer-shaped flowers in a wide range of colours throughout the summer. Easy to grow in most soils, it prefers a sunny position; its only drawback is that it is uninteresting when not in flower.

1.2m · 1.2m

≣ leaf type   ● light preference   ♨ speed of growth   ⚘ ease of growth

SAMBUCUS NIGRA
ELDER
CAPRIFOLIACEAE

Elder is a native plant that will thrive in any garden; it produces clusters of foamy cream flowers in midsummer followed by deep purple berries in autumn. Birds like robins, blackbirds and thrushes eat the elderberries. There are also gold, variegated and purple-leaved cultivars. Grow in most soils.

SYRINGA VULGARIS
LILAC
OLEACEAE

One of the most spectacular large shrubs for late spring flowering, the small scented flowers are single or double and tightly clustered in cone-shaped panicles. The common lilac is a rather dull pale lilac, but there are very attractive cultivars with white, cream, red or purple coloured flowers. It likes most soils.

ULEX EUROPAEUS 'FLORE PLENO'
GORSE
PAPILIONACEAE

Gorse is a familiar sight in the countryside, with spiky bushes covered in yellow pea flowers all summer long. This double-flowered variety is a more attractive garden plant. Plant in well-drained, sandy soil in the middle of beds and borders where the spikes will not be a problem.

VIBURNUM OPULUS 'STERILE'
GUELDER ROSE
CAPRIFOLIACEAE

A native shrub that is popular as a garden plant, which has attractive leaves that turn orange and yellow in autumn. This is the best cultivar for the garden, with large balls of white flowers covering the branches in summer. Grow in fertile, moist but well-drained soil.

VIBURNUM TINUS
LAURUSTINUS
CAPRIFOLIACEAE

An attractive, winter-flowering, evergreen shrub that will grow almost anywhere. The small white flowers are pink in bud and form loose domes that appear from autumn through to spring. The only problem is that they may suffer in extremely cold weather. Grow in most soils.

WEIGELA FLORIDA 'VARIEGATA'
WEIGELA
CAPRIFOLIACEAE

One of the best and easiest shrubs to grow, it deserves a place in every garden. A neat rounded bush with funnel-shaped pink flowers from late spring to midsummer. There are a range of good forms including excellent purple and green-and-white variegated-leaved varieties. It will grow in most soils.

---

height and spread   feature of interest   season of interest   *SHRUBS* **F – W**

85

ROSES

ROSA 'FLOWER CARPET'
ROSE
ROSACEAE

A great rose for the novice gardener as it seems to grow unaffected by any of the pests and diseases that damage other roses. It has shiny, almost evergreen leaves, low spreading branches, and bright pink flowers for most of the summer. Try it in a large pot on the patio. Grows in most soils.

75cm / 80cm

ROSA 'GRAHAM THOMAS'
ROSE
ROSACEAE

The English roses need less pruning and general care than the Floribunda and Hybrid Teas, but have the same large flowers and flower continuously. 'Graham Thomas' has large, cupped, double, deep yellow flowers with a rich, old rose fragrance and is one of the most reliable of the English roses. Grows in most soils.

1.2m / 80cm

ROSA 'ICEBERG'
ROSE
ROSACEAE

The finest and best white Floribunda rose, with clusters of pink-tinged buds opening to lightly scented white flowers and glossy green leaves that stay on the bushes into the winter. Flowers throughout the summer, and its only requirements are an annual light prune, a little food and the odd spray. Grows in most soils.

90cm / 60cm

ROSA 'JUST JOEY'
ROSE
ROSACEAE

One of the very best Hybrid Tea roses, 'Just Joey' is almost perfect, with large, fragrant, coppery-orange flowers from early summer to late autumn, and dark green, disease-resistant foliage. Like all Hybrid Teas, it needs annual pruning and feeding, and may need spraying from time to time. Grows in most soils.

90cm / 60cm

ROSA 'NEVADA'
ROSE
ROSACEAE

To really enjoy 'Nevada' at its best you need plenty of room. It needs at least 3m (10ft) but the reward is a rounded bush of elegantly arching branches covered in large, creamy blooms in June and September. It needs no pruning and infrequent spraying. Grows in most soils.

2m / 1.5m

ROSA 'PENELOPE'
ROSE
ROSACEAE

'Penelope' has everything you could want in a rose except small size: it needs to be allowed to grow unpruned to show its true potential, which is large clusters of semi-double, palest pink, beautifully scented flowers that repeat flower from June to November, and disease-resistant shiny leaves. It likes most soils.

1.5m / 1.5m

🍃 leaf type	⬤ light preference	⚘ speed of growth	⚙ ease of growth

CONIFERS

CHAMAECYPARIS LAWSONIANA 'PEMBURY BLUE'
LAWSON'S CYPRESS
CUPRESSACEAE
Probably the easiest of the 'blue' conifers to grow, Lawson's cypress is unfussy about soil, and grows relatively quickly. 'Pembury Blue' has neat, silvery-blue foliage, and initially forms an upright bush that develops into a columnar tree. It will tolerate most soils.

CHAMAECYPARIS PISIFERA 'BOULEVARD'
SAWARA CYPRESS
CUPRESSACEAE
Usually bought as a dwarf conifer, 'Boulevard' can ultimately grow to over 4m (13ft)! The steel-blue foliage is more open and feathery than 'Pembury Blue' and the plant grows into a more globular shape. Easy to grow, its preference is for moist soils that are not too heavy.

CRYPTOMERIA JAPONICA 'ELEGANS'
JAPANESE CEDAR
TAXODIACEAE
A conifer that merits a place in the shrub border for its attractive green foliage that turns copper-bronze during the winter. It also makes a good specimen tree or container plant, remaining attractive throughout the year. It is easy to grow in all but very dry conditions. Grow in any well-drained soil.

JUNIPERUS X PFITZERIANA
PFITZER JUNIPER
CUPRESSACEAE
Not for very small gardens, but a wonderful architectural ground-covering conifer where there is space. Unfussy as to soil, it is, unlike many other conifers, happy in shade. One word of warning: the plant is prickly to touch and so best positioned where children will not reach it. Grow in any well-drained soil.

THUJA OCCIDENTALIS 'RHEINGOLD'
WHITE CEDAR
CUPRESSACEAE
If you want a golden conifer, 'Rheingold' is your best choice, with old-gold-coloured foliage turning a rich copper-gold in winter, which adds a warmth to even the coldest garden. The white cedar is a very tolerant, easy-to-grow conifer but prefers soils that are not too wet.

THUJA PLICATA 'ZEBRINA'
WESTERN RED CEDAR
CUPRESSACEAE
This is another easy-to-grow, vigorous conifer that eventually makes a large tree. The foliage is light green striped with yellow-green and makes an interesting specimen plant for medium to large gardens. It tolerates almost all soils and conditions, including high alkalinity and extreme cold.

⌀ height and spread　　✳ feature of interest　　season of interest　　*ROSES, CONIFERS*

CLIMBERS

CLEMATIS MONTANA
CLEMATIS
RANUNCULACEAE

A rampant, twining climber that will grow almost anywhere, but needs the support of wires, a trellis or a pergola. The large, starry flowers that smother the plant in spring can be pink or white, and the shiny foliage is green or bronze, depending on the variety selected. Grow in fertile, well-drained soil.

HYDRANGEA ANOMALA PETIOLARIS
CLIMBING HYDRANGEA
HYDRANGEACEAE

The best self-clinging climber for shady walls and buildings; it has bright green leaves appearing early in the year and dome-shaped clusters of white flowers in summer. It is rather slow to start, and so it is worth buying a well-grown specimen in the first place. Grows in any soil.

JASMINUM OFFICINALIS
COMMON JASMINE
OLEACEAE

Another easy, vigorous climber with dark green leaves and clusters of sweetly scented white flowers from mid-summer to early autumn. Happy in sun or light shade, it can be used to lighten a partially shaded wall or to grow up an old apple tree, over a seat or through a trellis. Grow in fertile, well-drained soil.

LATHYRUS ODORATUS
SWEET PEA
PAPILIONACEAE

Sweet peas are easy to grow as long as you remember to soak the seed overnight before sowing. Children will probably prefer the older, taller varieties which they can grow into 'wigwams' using bamboo supports. There are also dwarf varieties that need no staking at all. Grow in fertile, well-drained soil.

LONICERA JAPONICA 'HALLIANA'
JAPANESE HONEYSUCKLE
CAPRIFOLIACEAE

Maybe the best honeysuckle, being easy and fast-growing, with twining stems, semi-evergreen leaves and clusters of creamy, richly scented flowers throughout summer. It is so rampant that it is best kept away from walls and grown over pergolas and other structures. Grow in fertile, moist, well-drained soil.

LONICERA PERICLYMENUM
COMMON HONEYSUCKLE, WOODBINE
CAPRIFOLIACEAE

One of our best-loved climbing plants, producing tubular florets, the base of each filled with nectar. The flowers are visited by bumble bees and a whole range of beautiful butterflies; later the fruits provide food for warblers, thrushes and bullfinches. Grow in fertile, moist but well-drained soil.

leaf type   light preference   speed of growth   ease of growth

PARTHENOCISSUS QUINQUEFOLIA
VIRGINIA CREEPER
VITACEAE

One of the favourite climbers for climbing up brick walls of old houses, where its brilliant scarlet autumn colour is unsurpassable. It is self-clinging so does not need the help of wires or a trellis. The five-fingered leaves are the major feature, the flowers being insignificant. Grows in almost any soil.

ROSA 'NEW DAWN'
ROSE
ROSACEAE

If you have room for just one rose, this might be it. Clusters of small, pink, fragrant flowers are produced throughout summer and autumn on long shoots that can be trained up a pillar or trellis, or left free to scramble over other shrubs in a large border. It has good disease resistance and grows in most soils.

ROSA 'ZEPHIRINE DROUHIN'
ROSE
ROSACEAE

A very old rose variety, with semi-double, cerise-pink, fragrant flowers and grey-green leaves and, as a bonus, practically no thorns! It flowers through the summer and is happy on a north-facing wall, where it seems less susceptible to mildew, which is one of its few problems. Grows in most soils.

THUNBERGIA ALATA
BLACKEYED SUSAN
ACANTHACEAE

A climber for the conservatory that can be treated as an annual in the garden if planted in a sunny, sheltered site. The plant will twine up posts or trail over banks, producing showy orange flowers above its arrow-shaped leaves. Grow in any well-drained, fertile soil.

TROPAEOLUM MAJUS
NASTURTIUM
TROPAEOLACEAE

Select nasturtiums as climbers to cover a trellis or fences, as trailing plants for windowboxes and containers, or as compact plants for growing in beds and borders. The large seeds should be individually sown in the soil or a container in the spring. These annuals need well-drained, moderately fertile soil.

WISTERIA FLORIBUNDA
JAPANESE WISTERIA
PAPILIONACEAE

Wisteria is attractive in all seasons, with contorted twining stems in winter, large, hanging racemes of violet-blue flowers in late spring, and fresh green leaves in summer. The flowers are beautifully scented, so put plants beneath a window, or over an arbour where they are at 'nose level'. Grows in most soils.

⇕ height and spread   ✳ feature of interest   � season of interest   CLIMBERS **C – W**

TREES

ACER PLATANOIDES 'CRIMSON KING'
PURPLE-LEAVED NORWAY MAPLE
ACERACEAE

A medium to large tree with large, shiny, dark purple leaves that become even more colourful in the autumn with red and orange tints. An extremely tolerant, easy-to-grow, vigorous tree whose only problem is its ability to outgrow the space allocated. It likes fertile, moist but well-drained soil.

16m / 11m

AMELANCHIER LAMARCKII
SNOWY MESPILIS
ROSACEAE

Amelanchiers are often seen as shrubs in gardens, but this species is available on a single stem to be grown as a small tree. Clouds of starry white flowers in spring are followed by neat, soft green leaves that turn red and orange in the autumn. Small enough to be found a space in every garden. Grow in well-drained soil.

8m / 6m

BETULA PENDULA 'YOUNGII'
YOUNG'S WEEPING BIRCH
BETULACEAE

A lovely dome-shaped tree, with weeping branches and a white stem. The triangular leaves have long stalks and turn yellow in autumn, and catkins hang down from the branches in early spring. It is best used as a specimen tree planted by a pond or to hang over a gate. Grow in moist but well-drained soil.

8m / 10m

MALUS HUPEHENSIS
FLOWERING CRAB APPLE
ROSACEAE

Crab apples are a very suitable choice of tree for a family garden, with their masses of pink blossom in late spring and attractive fruits in the autumn. *Malus hupehensis* is one of the prettiest with fragrant flowers and yellow and red fruits that can be made into crab apple jelly. Grow in well-drained, fertile soil.

8m / 6m

MALUS 'ROYALTY'
PLUM-LEAVED CRAB APPLE
ROSACEAE

If you want a purple-leaved tree that will not grow too large then select a plum-leaved crab apple, with clusters of wine-red flowers in spring and purple foliage all summer. 'Royalty' is the best form, with wine-coloured foliage and large, purple-red crab apples in autumn. Grow in well-drained, fertile soil.

8m / 6m

PRUNUS AVIUM 'PLENA'
DOUBLE-FLOWERED GEAN
ROSACEAE

The easiest to grow of the flowering cherries, and ideal for a medium-sized or larger garden. This is the double-flowered form of our native cherry, with hanging, pure white, double flowers in late spring. The green leaves turn yellow in autumn. This is a very popular street tree and ideal for avenues. Grow in any soil.

12m / 12m

🍃 leaf type	⬤ light preference	⚘ speed of growth	✿ ease of growth

PRUNUS SUBHIRTELLA 'AUTUMNALIS'
WINTER FLOWERING CHERRY
ROSACEAE

This is the only tree that flowers in the middle of winter, and it deserves to be grown in all but the very smallest garden. The pale pink blossoms open in late autumn on the bare branches and flower until early spring. The leaves appear after the flowers have fallen, and usually turn yellow in autumn. Grow in any soil.

7m / 7m

PYRUS CALLERYANA 'CHANTICLEER'
PEAR
ROSACEAE

This pear deserves to be grown far more than it is, as it has almost no faults. Easy to grow in almost any conditions, and with a neat upright habit, it has shiny green leaves which remain almost until winter is over, and white, cup-shaped blossoms that cover the whole tree in spring. Grow in any soil.

10m / 6m

PYRUS SALICIFOLA 'PENDULA'
WEEPING WILLOW-LEAVED PEAR
ROSACEAE

Another pear but quite different, with soft, silvery-grey leaves and weeping branches. The white blossoms appear with the leaves and are often followed by hard, inedible fruits in late summer. The long branches tend to grow untidily but it can easily be pruned into shape when necessary. Grow in any soil.

6m / 5m

SORBUS ARIA 'LUTESCENS'
WHITEBEAM
ROSACEAE

The whitebeam is one of the best trees for a medium-sized garden. It has a beautifully rounded shape, even when young, and large, round, grey-green leaves with white undersides. The dome-shaped clusters of creamy flowers are followed by bunches of bright red berries. It is excellent for chalky soils.

12m / 8m

SORBUS AUCUPARIA
ROWAN
ROSACEAE

Our native rowan is an attractive small tree, with clusters of fluffy white flowers in late spring followed by bright red fruits in autumn that are much enjoyed by birds. There is a yellow-berried cultivar 'Xanthocarpa', but birds seem to disregard the fruits. Grow in moderately fertile, well-drained soil.

15m / 9m

SORBUS 'JOSEPH ROCK'
ROSACEAE

A lovely, neat tree for the smaller garden with green leaves that turn yellow and orange in the autumn. Clusters of white flowers in early summer are followed by hanging bunches of yellow fruit that remain most of the winter as they seem to be less attractive to birds than red fruits. It is ideal for chalky conditions.

10m / 5m

⬍ height and spread   ✳ feature of interest   ▭ season of interest   *TREES* **A – S**

VEGETABLES AND FRUIT

ALLIUM AMPELOPRASUM VAR. PORRUM
LEEKS
ALLIACEAE

Leeks are one of the easiest members of the onion family to grow. However, grown from seed they will need transplanting, so for ease try to find leek plants that can be planted where they are to be harvested in the following winter. 'Musselburgh' is one of the best to look for. Grow in fertile, moisture-retentive soil.

ALLIUM CEPA
ONIONS
ALLIACEAE

Onions from seed take some care, as they will need thinning and transplanting, but grown from sets you have none of these problems. Just plant and then lift the fully grown onions twenty weeks later. 'Ailsa Craig' and 'Sturon' are both tried and tested favourites. Grow in fertile, well-drained soil.

ALLIUM CEPA
SPRING ONIONS
ALLIACEAE

Spring or salad onions are immature and mild-flavoured onions lifted young and used in salads. The seeds can be sown for pulling and eating eight weeks later, with successional sowings giving crops throughout the summer. The best and most popular salad variety is 'White Lisbon'. Grow in fertile, well-drained soil.

BETA VULGARIS (CICLA GROUP)
SWISS CHARD
CHENOPODIACEAE

Another plant whose leaves and stems are attractive enough to merit a place in the flower border rather than the vegetable garden. Sow in spring and start picking off the outside leaves from late summer through the autumn. There is a very attractive ruby chard with bright red stems. Grow in non-acid, fertile soil.

BETA VULGARIS SUBSP. VULGARIS
BEETROOT
CHENOPODIACEAE

An easy plant to grow – just sow the seeds in seed drills in the vegetable garden from mid-April for harvesting in July. Alternatively, the red stems and shiny leaves are attractive enough to include in beds and borders. Good varieties include 'Bonel' and 'Boltardy'. Grow in rich, well-drained soil.

BRASSICA OLERACEA (ACEPHALA GROUP)
KALE
BRASSICACEAE

Kale is a great crop for the novice vegetable gardener: it tolerates poor soils and frosts and appears untouched by pigeons, club root and cabbage root fly. The crop can be rather bitter, but using a variety like 'Dwarf Green Curled' and picking the leaves young lessens this problem. Grow in well-drained soil.

≣ leaf type   ● light preference   � speed of growth   ✿ ease of growth

BRASSICA OLERACEA (GEMMIFERA GROUP)
BRUSSELS SPROUTS
BRASSICACEAE

Not all children enjoy the flavour of Brussels sprouts, but they are a valuable vegetable for winter harvesting, and cooking sprouts fresh from the garden may change their minds. Use an F1 hybrid like 'Peer Gynt', which is one of the best varieties suitable for small gardens. Grow in fertile soil.

90cm / 75cm

BRASSICA OLERACEA (ITALICA GROUP)
BROCCOLI
BRASSICACEAE

Garden varieties are usually purple-sprouting broccoli rather than the green calabrese on sale in shops. This is an easier crop to grow than either the green form or the related white winter cauliflower. Sow in April or buy plants in September for planting out; harvest in January. Grow in fertile soil.

90cm / 30cm

CUCURBITA SPP.
GOURDS
CUCURBITACEAE

Gourds, which are very similar to marrows, are grown for the interesting colours and shapes of the ripe fruit, which can be picked, dried and varnished for use as ornaments. Sow a few seeds in late spring, water and feed well, and then harvest after ten to fourteen weeks.

45cm / 1m

CUCURBITA PEPO
MARROWS
CUCURBITACEAE

Marrows have a place in a children's vegetable garden for the sheer pleasure of cutting your name in the baby marrow and watching it enlarge as the marrow ripens. Plant in fertile soil, and select a variety like 'Green Bush' so that the immature marrows can be eaten as courgettes.

50cm / 2m

CUCURBITA PEPO
PUMPKINS
CUCURBITACEAE

Pumpkins are similar to marrows and gourds but produce enormous round orange fruit that are essential for Hallowe'en. 'Hundredweight' is a popular variety, but for giant pumpkins try 'Atlantic Giant'. Grow in fertile soil that is rich in humus, well drained, yet moisture-retentive.

50cm / 2m

CYNARA SCOLYMUS
GLOBE ARTICHOKE
ASTERACEAE

The large grey leaves and great thistle-like flowers of globe artichokes are attractive enough to warrant a place in the flower border rather than the vegetable garden, and this may be the best place as this vegetable needs plenty of room. The flower is harvested before it opens. Grow in fertile, well-drained soil.

1.8m / 1m

⇕ height and spread   ✳ feature of interest   ▮▮▮ season of interest   *VEGETABLES AND FRUIT* **A – C**

VEGETABLES AND FRUIT

DAUCUS CAROTA
CARROTS
APIACEAE

Carrots are one of the easiest vegetables to grow, with the feathery leaves emerging two weeks after sowing and the carrot roots developing almost as quickly, with fully grown carrots being ready to lift twelve weeks after sowing. Carrots are a good starting crop for impatient young gardeners. Grow in fertile soil.

FRAGARIA VESCA
ALPINE STRAWBERRIES
ROSACEAE

These low-growing perennial plants produce small, sweet strawberries throughout the summer; birds tend to ignore them. Once planted they are easy to grow, and can be left in place for several years. 'Baron Solemacher' is one of the best varieties. Grow in moist but well-drained, fertile, neutral to alkaline soil.

LACTUCA SATIVA
LETTUCE
ASTERACEAE

Lettuce is another good crop for the young impatient gardener, with many of the loose-leaf varieties being cut only six weeks after sowing. Sow any time from late spring through the summer on well-fertilized soil. 'Tom Thumb' is a good, fast-growing variety, or start with a packet of mixed lettuce seed.

LYCOPERSICON ESCULENTUM
TOMATOES
SOLANACEAE

Although not the easiest plants to grow, tomatoes are still a firm favourite for the family garden. Choose a bushy variety such as 'Little Wonder', which can be grown in a container and does not need supports. Grow in fertile soil – dig in plenty of well-rotted manure before planting.

PHASEOLUS COCCINEUS
RUNNER BEANS
PAPILIONACEAE

Included here for the pleasure of growing up trellises, over playhouses or 'wigwams' of bamboo, runner beans are a favourite with most children. The bright red flowers are followed by long bean pods that offer the chance of a competition for growing the longest bean. Grow in fertile soil that retains moisture.

PHASEOLUS VULGARIS
FRENCH BEANS
PAPILIONACEAE

Ready before runner beans and without the need for supports, French beans are a useful and relatively easy plant to grow in the summer vegetable garden. Sow direct as soon as the last frosts are over in any but a heavy clay or acid soil. There are novel varieties with yellow and purple pods.

| leaf type | light preference | speed of growth | ease of growth |

PISUM SATIVUM

PEAS

PAPILIONACEAE

The flavour of young, newly shelled peas is deliciously sweet. You can also grow mangetout or sugar peas which are eaten in the pod and so eliminate the need for shelling. Grow in moisture-retentive but well-drained soil, and incorporate plenty of well-rotted manure before planting.

50cm–1.5m
15cm

RAPHANUS SATIVUS

RADISHES

BRASSICACEAE

Even faster growing than carrots, radishes can be ready for lifting about a month after sowing, and are ideal for children to grow even if they are not absolutely sure about the peppery taste. 'French Breakfast' is an excellent, mild-flavoured variety, but needs lifting young. Grow in rich, well-drained soil.

1.5m
1.5m

RUMEX ACETOSA

SORREL

POLYGONACEAE

A good plant to grow as a 'cut and come again' salad vegetable. The lemony flavour of the leaves is a delicious addition to salads or soups. A perennial plant, it can be left over winter for cutting in subsequent years or grown annually from seed. It needs a well-drained, fertile soil enriched with added humus.

30–80cm
45cm

SOLANUM TUBEROSUM

POTATOES

SOLANACEAE

To keep the family in potatoes all year through requires more space in our gardens than is often available, but they are a useful crop for cleaning the ground and it is worthwhile at least growing early potatoes. Grow in well-drained, fertile soil that is at least 60cm (2ft) deep.

45cm
30cm

VICIA FABA

BROAD BEANS

PAPILIONACEAE

A vegetable that the whole family can enjoy growing, with the younger members having fun watching the large seeds germinate and later helping to strip off the beans' 'fur' coats. There is a good dwarf variety, 'The Sutton'. Broad beans are not fussy about soil as long as it is well drained.

30cm–1.8m
30cm

ZEA MAYS

SWEET CORN

POACEAE

Sweet corn needs to wait for the last of the frosts before sowing, but, given a warm summer, the giant stems grow amazingly quickly, and the tassels of the flowers and the ripening cobs are fascinating to young gardeners. The cobs should be ready for harvesting fourteen weeks after sowing. Grow in fertile soil.

1.5–2m
45cm

⬍ height and spread   ✳ feature of interest   ▭▭▭ season of interest   *VEGETABLES AND FRUIT* **D – Z**

HERBS

ALLIUM SCHOENOPRASUM
CHIVES
ALLIACEAE

Chives make an ideal edging to the vegetable plot, with their neat clumps of grass-like leaves and round heads of pink flowers. Add the onion-flavoured leaves to soups, salads and sandwiches, and use the flowers to decorate salads. Sow seeds direct or use small plants. Grow in well-drained or moist soil.

ANETHUM GRAVEOLENS
DILL
APIACEAE

The fine feathery leaves and small yellow-green flowers look like fennel, and if grown together the two plants may hybridize. Sow the seeds into pots or the ground where the crop is to grow, and cut fresh leaves to use with fish dishes or harvest the seeds to add to pickling vinegar. Grow in a fertile, well-drained soil.

ANGELICA ARCHANGELICA
ANGELICA
APIACEAE

With large cut leaves and elegant stems carrying round balls of flowers, angelica is a plant that makes a statement wherever it is planted. The young cut stems make the crystallized cake decoration, and the leaves and stems can be stewed with fruit. Finches love to eat the seeds. Grow deep in moist, fertile soil.

ANTHRISCUS CEREFOLIUM
CHERVIL
APIACEAE

A hardy annual which, if sown late in the summer, acts as a biennial and will provide leaves for cutting during the winter before coming into flower and then dying the next year. The fresh green fern-like leaves are cut for use in salads, soups, sauces and with vegetables. Grow in well-drained or moist soil.

ARTEMISIA DRACUNCULUS
TARRAGON
ASTERACEAE

Not a particularly attractive plant, but a 'must' for all keen cooks. Check that you plant French tarragon and not the Russian form which is larger and practically tasteless. Once established, pick young leaves from the plant for using fresh from June to October. Grow in well-drained, fertile soil.

BORAGO OFFICINALIS
BORAGE
BORAGINACEAE

An annual with bright blue, star-shaped flowers and furry leaves and stems that have a cucumber-like flavour. It grows very easily from seed and will happily self-seed and come up year after year. The flowers can be used in salads and summer drinks and are visited by bees for pollen and nectar. Grow in any soil.

leaf type   light preference   speed of growth   ease of growth

CARUM CARVI
CARAWAY
APIACEAE

This plant has fern-like leaves and small white flowers that produce aromatic seeds which are used to flavour cakes, bread, vegetables and stews. The roots can be cooked as a vegetable if left to the second autumn after sowing. Easy to grow from seed in any reasonable, well-drained soil.

60cm / 30cm

CORIANDRUM SATIVUM
CORIANDER
APIACEAE

An increasingly popular herb with both the leaves and seeds being used in cooking. Sow the seeds in late spring or early summer where they are to grow as coriander dislikes being transplanted. Avoid growing in damp or humid areas as it needs dry conditions to crop well.

60cm / 30cm

FOENICULUM VULGARE
FENNEL
APIACEAE

Fennel forms tall drifts of feathery foliage topped by flat domes of tiny yellow flowers in the late summer. Plant either in a herb garden or at the back of a border. There is a bronze-leaved cultivar, 'Purpureum', that is even more attractive and just as useful in the kitchen. Grow in fertile, moist, well-drained soil.

1.8m / 45cm

HYSSOPUS OFFICINALIS
HYSSOP
LAMIACEAE

A very pretty herb with upright stems of aromatic dark green leaves and spikes of blue or pink flowers. Traditionally used in the treatment of whooping cough and chest ailments, it is now used as an edging plant or a low hedge. Popular with both butterflies and bees. Grow in fertile, well-drained soil.

45cm / 45cm

LAURUS NOBILIS
SWEET BAY
LAURACEAE

An evergreen plant that can be trained to form a mop-headed tree, clipped as a rounded bush, or left unclipped to grow into a large shrub. There is a golden-leaved cultivar, 'Aureum', that can be used to brighten up a shady corner. The leaves of both can be used in cooking. Grow in fertile, moist but well-drained soil.

10m / 6m

LAVANDULA ANGUSTIFOLIA
LAVENDER
LAMIACEAE

There are lots of different lavenders for the gardener to grow, and all form rounded bushes with spikes of aromatic flowers in all shades of lavender blue but also white and pink. It is a very important plant for both bees and butterflies. All varieties need well-drained, preferably limey soil in full sun.

60cm / 60cm

⬍ height and spread   ✳ feature of interest   ▭ season of interest   *HERBS A – L*

HERBS

MELISSA OFFICINALIS
LEMON BALM
LAMIACEAE

A wonderfully lemon-scented perennial that will grow almost anywhere. It has bright green, deeply veined leaves and small white flowers in summer, and there is a really lovely form with yellow and green variegated leaves called 'Aurea'. It is an excellent plant for a container. It likes any well-drained soil.

90cm / 45cm

MENTHA PIPERITA
PEPPERMINT
LAMIACEAE

This mint has dark stems and pointed deep green leaves and purple flowers. It smells strongly of peppermint and is used to make peppermint tea which is an aid to digestion. As with all mints, its roots need to be contained to avoid becoming a nuisance. It prefers moist soil.

45-60cm

MENTHA SPICATA
SPEARMINT
LAMIACEAE

This is the mint to use for mint sauce, and like all the mints it is a rampant perennial with shiny green leaves and pale purple flowers in summer. Plant in a container on the terrace or in an open-bottomed pot sunk into the ground to keep the roots under control. Grow in poor, moist soil.

90cm / 60cm

MYRRHIS ODORATUS
SWEET CICELY
APIACEAE

One of the first herbs to appear in the spring with fern-like leaves which smell of aniseed and have a sugary taste. Clusters of small white flowers follow in summer. The leaves can be chopped into salads and omelettes or used to sweeten stewed fruit. Grow in moist soil.

60-90cm / 60cm

OCIMUM BASILICUM
BASIL
LAMIACEAE

A tender perennial usually treated as an annual with bright green leaves and white flowers. Buy and plant out after all danger of frost is over, or keep in a pot on the windowsill. There is an attractive purple-leaved form, 'Purpurascens', with pink flowers. Grow in fertile, well-drained soil.

45cm / 20cm

ORIGANUM VULGARE
MARJORAM
LAMIACEAE

A perennial with soft evergreen leaves and violet flowers in mid-summer. Easy to grow, marjoram is an attractive plant for the front of the flower border, in a pot, or in the herb garden. Look for the golden marjoram 'Aureum', which will brighten up the dullest of gardens. Grow in poor, well-drained soil.

40cm / 45cm

≡ leaf type   ● light preference   ♣ speed of growth   ⚙ ease of growth

PETROSELINUM CRISPUM
PARSLEY
APIACEAE

A biennial with bright green, curly leaves that are a popular garnish for salads and sandwiches. It makes a useful edging plant in sun or part shade, and lasts longer if well watered and if any potential flowers are removed before opening. Grow in moist but well-drained, fertile soil.

75cm / 20cm

ROSMARINUS OFFICINALIS
ROSEMARY
LAMIACEAE

One of the best herbs, with aromatic, evergreen grey leaves and pale blue flowers in spring and intermittently throughout the year. It can be grown in a pot, in the herb garden, or as a gentle foil to a colourful mixed border. There are a range of interesting cultivars. Grow in well-drained soil.

1.5m / 1.5m

SALVIA OFFICINALIS
COMMON SAGE
LAMIACEAE

An aromatic evergreen shrub with large, velvety, grey-green leaves and clusters of pale purple flowers for most of the summer. It is an excellent front to mid-border shrub, and there are also gold, purple and tri-coloured leaved cultivars. Grow in humus-rich, well-drained soil.

80cm / 60cm

SATUREJA MONTANA
WINTER SAVORY
LAMIACEAE

An evergreen sub-shrub, winter savory is a useful plant for the herb garden, and available all year round. The low bushes have dark green leaves and rather insignificant white flowers in mid-summer that are very popular with bees. Grow in neutral to alkaline, well-drained and moderately fertile soil.

30cm / 20cm

THYMUS X CITRIODORUS
LEMON THYME
LAMIACEAE

A dwarf evergreen sub-shrub that makes a lovely ground cover for a warm, sunny corner, or for gaps in a paved area. Lemon thyme has lemon-scented leaves that can be used in cooking. There are gold-and-silver-leaved forms which are even more ornamental. Grow in well-drained soil.

30cm / 30cm

THYMUS VULGARIS
GARDEN THYME
LAMIACEAE

Garden or common thyme is similar to lemon thyme but has a herbal fragrance and smaller, darker leaves. The leaves are used in stews, salads and sauces, and the mauve flowers are very attractive to bees. There are a range of cultivars with coloured leaves. Grow in well-drained soil.

30cm / 30cm

↕ height and spread   ✱ feature of interest   ▭ season of interest   *HERBS* **M – T**

PLANTS THAT CAN CAUSE SKIN RASHES

ALSTROEMERIA 'LIGTU HYBRIDS'
PERUVIAN LILY
ALSTROEMERIACEAE
These plants have narrow, twisted, pale green leaves with very pretty flowers looking like clusters of small lilies, in a range of soft colours from pink to pale yellow and apricot. Be careful when handling the plants because repeated contact may cause allergic dermatitis. Grow in fertile, moist but well-drained soil.

90cm / 45cm

ARUM ITALICUM
LORDS AND LADIES
ARACEAE
A plant of our woodlands that is often found in gardens. It has arrow-shaped leaves and sheath-like flowers followed by bright orange berries that are very attractive to children. All parts of the plant, but particularly the berries, are poisonous, and the sap is a skin and eye irritant. Grow in humus-rich, well-drained soil.

30cm / 15cm

DAPHNE LAUREOLA
SPURGE LAUREL
THYMELAEACEAE
A low, evergreen, winter-flowering shrub that is useful in the garden for planting in shady areas. The yellow, scented flowers are in rounded clusters followed by black fruit. Unfortunately, the sap and berries are poisonous, and the sap also causes dermatitis. Grow in humus-rich, moderately fertile soil.

90cm / 90cm

DAPHNE MEZEREUM
MEZEREON
THYMELAEACEAE
A very popular shrub, with bright pink, scented flowers that appear on the bare stems in early spring. These are followed in late summer by bright red poisonous berries. Both the sap and the juice of the berries can cause dermatitis, so it is not a plant for the family garden.

80cm / 1m

DICTAMNUS ALBUS
BURNING BUSH
RUTACEAE
An interesting plant with tall spikes of pink and white flowers above deeply divided foliage. The ripening seed pods release a gas that burns when lit, giving it the familiar name of burning bush. Contact with the sap in sunny weather can cause a nasty skin rash. Grow in any dry, moderately fertile soil.

60cm / 45cm

ECHIUM PLANTAGINEUM
VIPER'S BUGLOSS
BORAGINACEAE
A native plant now grown as a popular bedding plant, with pretty blue and pink flowers and hairy stems. It is very easy to grow but children need to be warned that the hairs on the stems are highly irritant and can cause skin rashes. Grow in well-drained, moderately fertile soil.

30cm / 20cm

leaf type | light preference | speed of growth | ease of growth

EUPHORBIA SPP.
SPURGE
EUPHORBIACEAE

Spurges have become very popular with gardeners in recent years because they have foliage which is interesting all year round and extraordinary green-coloured flowers. Unfortunately, all euphorbias have a milky sap that is highly allergenic and can cause skin irritation and dermatitis. It likes well-drained soil.

80cm–1.2m
30–60cm

FICUS CARICA
FIG
MORACEAE

An attractive garden plant with large, beautifully lobed leaves. It cannot be relied on to produce fruit, but it will help if you select a variety like 'Brown Turkey' and keep the roots restricted. The plant sap can cause a severe reaction if it is in contact with the skin in sunny weather. It will grow in most soil.

4m
6m

FREMONTODENDRON CALIFORNICUM
FLANNEL BUSH
STERCULIACEAE

A lovely wall shrub for a warm sunny wall, with heart-shaped, grey-green leaves and saucer-shaped, yellow flowers all summer. All parts of the plant have tiny hairs that are extremely irritating and when touched may affect the skin, mouth, nose and eyes. Grow in poor, well-drained, neutral to alkaline soil.

6m
4m

HEDERA HELIX
COMMON IVY, ENGLISH IVY
ARALIACEAE

The most common of our climbing plants and capable of growing almost anywhere. It has evergreen leaves on self-clinging stems, and there is a range of variegated forms. The sap from all parts of the plant is harmful and may cause skin rashes, and all parts of the plant are poisonous. Grow in any soil.

6m

HERACLEUM MANTEGAZZIANUM
GIANT HOGWEED
APIACEAE

A quite magnificent native plant grown in gardens for its large, deeply divided leaves and its 3m (10ft) high stems topped with rounded heads of creamy flowers. The sap is extremely dangerous if allowed to touch the skin, and this plant should never be grown in gardens where there are children.

3m
1.5m

RUTA GRAVEOLENS
COMMON RUE
RUTACEAE

A low-growing evergreen shrub with small, blue-green leaves and open yellow flowers. It is one of the worst plants for causing skin damage and must be treated with extreme caution. Do not grow it in any garden where there are small children, and always handle with gloves.

1m
75cm

⬍ height and spread   ✳ feature of interest   ▭ season of interest   *IRRITANT PLANTS* **A – R**

PLANTS WITH THORNS AND PRICKLES

ARALIA SPINOSA

DEVIL'S WALKING STICK

ARALIACEAE

One of the thorniest plants to grow: the upright stems are covered in sharp pointed spines. The leaves are large and most attractively divided, and in summer feathery panicles of greeny-white flowers appear at the top of the stems. Treat with extreme care. It likes humus-rich, fertile, moist soil.

3m / 3m

BERBERIS THUNBERGII

BARBERRY

BERBERIDACEAE

All the barberries have prickly leaves and stems and need to be handled with great care. They do, however, make extremely good and impenetrable hedges – a useful deterrent to intruders. They all have attractive yellow flowers, and *Berberis thunbergii* has many coloured-leaved cultivars. It likes most soils.

2.4m / 2m

CHAENOMELES JAPONICA

JAPANESE QUINCE

ROSACEAE

A vigorous shrub with colourful, cup-shaped flowers in early spring before the leaves appear. Usually grown against a wall, large pear-shaped fruits often appear after a warm summer. It has sharp thorns, so place at the back of the border out of the reach of children. Grow in well-drained, moderately fertile soil.

3m / 2m

CRATAEGUS LAEVIGATA

HAWTHORN

ROSACEAE

All the hawthorns have very sharp thorns along their branches. They are, however, very attractive and easy-to-grow garden trees, and they also make very effective hedges. Place with care and prevent children trying to climb up specimens or using trees for tree-houses. Grow in any soil apart from a waterlogged one.

6m / 6m

GLEDITSIA TRIACANTHOS

HONEY LOCUST

CAESALPINACEAE

The honey locust has soft green leaves and white flowers, and there is a lovely yellow-leaved cultivar, 'Sunburst', which is often planted as a garden tree. However, the branches have branched spines, so place carefully or look for the spineless green-leaved cultivar 'Inermis'. Grow in any fertile soil.

14m / 10m

ILEX AQUIFOLIUM

COMMON HOLLY, ENGLISH HOLLY

AQUIFOLIACEAE

One of our few native evergreen trees, its red berries are an essential ingredient of Christmas. It also supports many insects and birds. Its prickly leaves are shed throughout the year, break down very slowly and can be a menace in a garden with children. Grow in moist but well-drained soil.

6.5m / 4m

SPRING SUMMER AUTUMN WINTER

| | leaf type | | light preference | | speed of growth | | ease of growth |

PONCIRUS TRIFOLIATA
JAPANESE BITTER ORANGE
RUTACEAE

An unusual plant with very sweetly scented, large, white flowers in mid-spring on almost leafless green branches that are armed with green spines 3cm (1¼in) long. Large yellow fruits appear later in the year. A choice plant for the keen gardener but not for the family garden. It likes fertile, well-drained soil.

3m / 3m

PRUNUS SPINOSA
SLOE
ROSACEAE

The twiggy branches of sloe are a mass of white blossom in early spring before the leaves appear. The purple fruit are used for making sloe gin. Sloe would have been included in the main section of this directory were it not for its very nasty black thorns which can be dangerous. Grow in any soil.

5m / 4m

PYRACANTHA 'MOHAVE'
FIRETHORN
ROSACEAE

A useful evergreen shrub, with clusters of white flowers in late spring and orange-red berries in the autumn. Best used trained against a shady wall but it is also a handsome shrub for the shrub border or wild garden. Sharp spines are found in the leaf axils so plant away from children's play areas. It likes most soils.

3m / 3m

ROBINIA PSEUDOACACIA
FALSE ACACIA, BLACK LOCUST
PAPILIONACEAE

Similar to the honey locust, with white flowers and bright green leaves, and there is an attractive yellow-leaved cultivar, 'Frisia'. However, the false acacia branches are covered in sharp thorns and it also has the nasty habit of dropping branches at random – so omit this from the family garden.

18m / 15m

ROSA SPP.
ROSE
ROSACEAE

There are two pages of roses already in this directory, but this section would be incomplete without including these, one of our thorniest and prickliest of garden plants. Some people are allergic to rose thorns and if you or your family suffer then perhaps you should avoid growing roses.

1–3m / 60cm–1.5m

RUBUS FRUTICOSUS
BRAMBLE
ROSACEAE

The bramble or blackberry with its delicious berries is one of our best native shrubs for wildlife and merits a place in all but the most formal of gardens. However, it is covered with small thorns, and children need to be taught to treat brambles with care. Grow in most soils.

up to 90cm / 3.6m

⬍ height and spread   ✳ feature of interest   ▭ season of interest   *THORNY PLANTS* **A – R**

103

POISONOUS PLANTS

ACONITUM NAPELLUS
MONKSHOOD
RANUNCULACEAE
A stately plant with tall spikes of blue hooded flowers and deeply divided leaves. This is one of the most poisonous of garden plants, containing aconitine throughout the plant but particularly in the roots. It is possible to absorb the poison through the skin, so remove it from your garden.

90cm–1.5m / 60cm

ATROPA BELLADONNA
DEADLY NIGHTSHADE
SOLANACEAE
A native plant that very rarely occurs as a weed in our gardens, but if it is found it must be removed and destroyed. The leaves are greyish-green and the dull, purplish, bell-like flowers appear in summer, followed by shiny black berries which are extremely poisonous and indeed 'deadly'.

1.2m / 30cm

BRYONIA DIOICA
WHITE BRYONY
CUCURBITACEAE
White bryony is commonly seen in the countryside climbing through hedgerows and it occasionally appears as a weed in the garden. The leaves have three or five pointed lobes, and the clusters of small greenish flowers are followed by dull red berries in the autumn. All parts are poisonous.

3m / 45cm

COLCHICUM AUTUMNALE
AUTUMN CROCUS
COLCHICACEAE
Unlike the more familiar Dutch crocus, colchicums flower in the autumn after the leaves have died down. Up to a dozen lilac, goblet-shaped flowers emerge from each corm, and there are both white and double-flowered varieties available. All parts of the plant are poisonous. It likes fertile, well-drained soil.

25cm / 10cm

CONVALLARIA MAJALIS
LILY OF THE VALLEY
CONVALLARIACEAE
A familiar favourite with beautifully scented, dainty, white, bell flowers and broad, dark green leaves, ideal for a shady part of the garden or for growing under trees and shrubs. Green berries, becoming red as they ripen, appear after the flowers. All parts of the plant are poisonous. It likes fertile, humus-rich soil.

15cm / 30cm

DATURA STRAMONIUM
THORNAPPLE
SOLANACEAE
Another very rare, but deadly plant, which is sometimes found as a weed and which should be carefully removed and destroyed if found in your garden. It has large irregularly pointed leaves and attractive, white, trumpet-shaped flowers and green spiny fruit which split into four segments.

1m / 45cm

≣ leaf type   ● light preference   ⚘ speed of growth   ✿ ease of growth

DIGITALIS PURPUREA
FOXGLOVE
SCROPHULARIACEAE

A common plant of woodland but now frequently grown in the garden, the foxglove has large hairy leaves and tall spikes of hanging purple or white tubular flowers and green fruits. All parts of the plant are poisonous, so remove all plants to avoid children playing with the flowers.

1.5m / 45cm

EUONYMUS EUROPAEUS
SPINDLE
CELASTRACEAE

There are various species of euonymus grown in the garden, but this is our native spindle, with deciduous leaves turning red in autumn. The flowers are insignificant but are followed by pink fleshy fruit that split open to reveal bright orange seeds. All parts of the plant are poisonous.

3m / 3m

HYOSCYAMUS NIGER
HENBANE
SOLANACEAE

Another rare, but dangerous, native plant that very occasionally is found as a garden weed. A very distinctive plant, it is covered in sticky hairs with thick stems, lobed leaves, yellowish funnel-shaped flowers and green fruits. All parts are extremely poisonous – remove on sight in the garden.

75cm / 45cm

IPOMOEA TRICOLOR
MORNING GLORY
CONVOLVULACEAE

Grown as an annual climber for its clear blue, trumpet flowers, which appear in the morning and die in the afternoon, but are replaced by more flowers that open the next day. Quite easy to grow from seed but the seeds contain a hallucinogenic substance and are dangerous if eaten. It likes most soils.

4m / 4m

LABURNUM ANAGYROIDES
GOLDEN RAIN TREE
PAPILIONACEAE

A small tree with hanging bunches of yellow flowers in spring, followed by green pods containing black, shiny, extremely poisonous seeds that are very attractive to children. A few seeds can prove fatal so never grow laburnums where there are young children. It will grow in most soils.

7m / 5m

LANTANA CAMARA
YELLOW SAGE
VERBENACEACE

This is usually grown as a conservatory plant brought out into the garden for the summer. A shrub with coarse, pointed leaves and round clusters of yellow, orange, pink or red flowers, the leaves, flowers, and particularly the unripe fruit are poisonous. Avoid growing it in the family garden.

2m / 2m

⬍ height and spread   ✳ feature of interest   ▭ season of interest   *POISONOUS PLANTS* **A – L**

POISONOUS PLANTS

LIGUSTRUM OVALIFOLIUM
PRIVET
OLEACEAE

One of the most popular plants for hedging, with evergreen, shiny leaves and fluffy, scented, cream flowers in summer. The flowers are followed by shiny black berries. There are cultivars with yellow and variegated leaves. The whole plant is poisonous, particularly the berries. It likes well-drained soils.

NERIUM OLEANDER
OLEANDER
APOCYNACEAE

Despite its beautiful appearance, with large clusters of pink or white flowers, this is an extremely dangerous plant: eating it can prove fatal and even inhaling the smoke from a fire on which it is being burnt can be dangerous. This is not a plant even to consider for the family garden.

OENANTHE CROCATA
HEMLOCK WATER DROPWORT
APIACEAE

Another dangerously poisonous wild plant that needs to be left alone but may occur as a weed in the wet areas of the garden. Its folk name is dead man's fingers as the roots are a bunch of white tubers. The leaves are deeply divided and the flowers are open domes of small white flowers.

PHYTOLACCA AMERICANA
POKEWEED
PHYTOLACCACEAE

An uncommon garden plant grown for its spikes of clustered, small, pinkish-white flowers that develop into large 'pokers' of juicy, purplish-black berries which look edible. All parts of the plant are poisonous, but particularly the roots, unripe berries and seeds. Do not grow it in the family garden.

PRUNUS LAUROCERASUS
CHERRY LAUREL
ROSACEAE

A useful evergreen with large, shiny leaves that makes a very effective hedge. The tall spikes of white flowers in spring are followed by columns of large red berries that gradually turn black and look like cherries. All parts of the plant are poisonous. It likes a soil that is moist, well-drained and moderately fertile.

RHAMNUS CATHARTICA
BUCKTHORN
RHAMNACEAE

Known as 'purging' buckthorn, for the effect of eating the twigs or fruits, this is a very common native plant of scrub, woodland or hedgerows, and is occasionally found as a weed in an overgrown garden. A nondescript thorny shrub with inconspicuous flowers, but shiny red then black berries.

≣ leaf type   ● light preference   ♣ speed of growth   ✿ ease of growth

RICINUS COMMUNIS
CASTOR-OIL PLANT
EUPHORBIACEAE

A very dramatic plant, with shiny red leaves frequently seen in summer bedding schemes. This is perhaps the most dangerous plant grown in our gardens, as handling the plant can cause sore skin and the whole plant, but particularly the seeds, contains a deadly poison. Never grow it in your family garden.

1.5m / 1m

SOLANUM DULCAMARA
WOODY NIGHTSHADE
SOLANACEAE

A native plant that can be found scrambling through hedgerows and small trees, but it is also planted in the garden for its attractive purple flowers each with a central yellow cone. The bunches of small round fruits are green and then red when ripe. The unripe fruits are particularly poisonous.

2m / 40cm

SOLANUM NIGRUM
BLACK NIGHTSHADE
SOLANACEAE

This annual is a common weed of wasteland and our gardens. The clusters of white, potato-like flowers are followed by bunches of shiny black berries. All parts of the plant are extremely poisonous, but particularly the unripe berries, so remove any plants you find in the garden and destroy them.

50cm / 30cm

TAMUS COMMUNIS
BLACK BRYONY
DIOSCOREACEAE

Another wild plant that can occasionally be found as a weed. A twining plant with glossy, heart-shaped leaves and clusters of greenish-yellow flowers, the fruit are round, shiny green berries that turn black when ripe. The sap is a severe irritant and all parts of the plant are poisonous.

3m / 45cm

TAXUS BACCATA
YEW
TAXACEAE

The best conifer for clipped hedges and the backbone of the formal garden, yew is almost indispensable with its shiny, dark green needles all year round and its bright red 'berries'. Unfortunately, the leaves and seeds are poisonous. It likes well-drained, fertile soil.

20m / 10cm

VERATRUM NIGRUM
FALSE HELLIBORINE
MELANTHIACEAE

A choice statuesque plant for the shady garden, with very large ribbed leaves and tall flower spikes of closely packed, dark red flowers. The small seed pods turn black as they ripen. All parts of the plant, but particularly the roots and leaves, are toxic. This is definitely not a plant to include in the family garden.

2m / 60cm

⭳ height and spread   ✳ feature of interest   ▭▭▭ season of interest   *POISONOUS PLANTS* **L – V**

GLOSSARY

ALPINE: A plant that in its natural mountain habitat grows above the uppermost limit of trees. More colloquially, plants that are suitable for rock gardens are called alpines.

ANNUAL: A plant that grows from seed, flowers and dies within the same year. Some half-hardy perennial plants are used as annuals, that is, they die off in the winter.

AQUATIC PLANT: A plant that lives totally or partly submerged in water.

AXIL: The upper angle between leaf and stem.

BEDDING PLANTS: Plants that are set out for a temporary spring or summer display and discarded at the end of the season.

BIENNIAL: A plant raised from seed that makes its initial growth in one year and flowers during the following one, then dies.

BOG GARDEN PLANTS: Plants that live with their roots in moist soil.

BULB: An underground food storage organ formed of fleshy, modified leaves that enclose a dormant shoot.

CALYX: The outer and protective part of a flower. It is usually green and is very apparent in roses.

COMPOST: Vegetable waste from kitchens, as well as soft parts of garden plants, which is encouraged to decompose and to form a material that can be dug into soil or used to create a mulch around plants.

CORM: An underground storage organ formed of a swollen stem base, for example, a gladiolus.

CULTIVAR: A shortened term for 'cultivated variety' that indicates a variety raised in cultivation. Strictly speaking, most modern varieties are cultivars, but the term variety is still widely used because it is familiar to most gardeners.

CUTTING: A section of plant which is detached and encouraged to form roots and stems to provide a new independent plant. Cuttings may be taken from roots, stems or leaves.

DEAD-HEADING: The removal of a faded flower head to prevent the formation of seeds and to encourage the development of further flowers.

DORMANT: When a plant is alive but is making no growth, it is called dormant. The dormant period is usually the winter.

EVERGREEN: Plants that appear to be green throughout the year and not to lose their leaves are called evergreen. In reality, however, they shed some of their leaves throughout the year, while producing others.

FRIABLE: Soil that is crumbly and light and easily worked. It especially applies to soil being prepared as a seedbed in spring.

HALF-HARDY: A plant that can withstand fairly low temperatures, but needs protection from frost.

HALF-HARDY ANNUAL: An annual that is sown in gentle warmth in a greenhouse in spring, the seedlings being transferred to wider spacings in pots or boxes. The plants are placed in a garden or container only when all risk of frost has passed.

HARDEN OFF: To gradually accustom plants raised under cover to cooler conditions so that they can be planted outside.

HARDY: A plant that is able to survive outdoors in winter. In the case of some rock-garden plants, good drainage is essential to ensure their survival.

HERB: A plant that is grown for its aromatic qualities and can often be used in cooking or medicinally.

HERBACEOUS PERENNIAL: A plant with no woody tissue that lives for several years. Herbaceous perennials may be deciduous or evergreen.

HYBRID: A cross between two different species, varieties or genera of plants.

LOAM: Friable topsoil.

MARGINAL PLANTS: Plants that live in shallow water at the edges of ponds. Some also thrive in boggy soil surrounding a pond.

MULCHING: Covering the soil around plants with well-decayed organic material such as garden compost, peat or, in the case of rock garden plants, stone chippings or 6mm (¼ in) shingle.

NEUTRAL: Soil that is neither acid nor alkaline, with a pH of 7.0, is said to be neutral. Most plants grow in a pH of about 6.5.

PEAT: A naturally occurring substance formed from partly rotted organic material in water logged soils, used as a growing medium and soil additive.

PERENNIAL: Any plant that lives for three or more years is called a perennial.

PERGOLA: An open timber structure made up of linked arches.

POTTING COMPOST: Traditionally, a compost formed of loam, sharp sand and peat, fertilizers and chalk. The ratio of the ingredients is altered according to whether the compost is used for sowing seeds, potting-up or repotting plants into larger containers. Recognition of the environmental importance of conserving peat beds has led to many modern composts being formed of other organic materials, such as coir or shredded bark.

PRICKING OFF: Transplanting seedlings from the container in which they were sown to one where they are more widely spaced.

RACEME: An elongated flower head with each flower having a stem.

RAISED BED: A raised area, usually encircled by a dry-stone wall. Rock garden plants can be grown both in the raised bed and the wall.

RHIZOME: An underground or partly buried horizontal stem. They can be slender or fleshy. Some irises have thick, fleshy rhizomes, while those of lily-of-the-valley are slender and creeping. They act as storage organs and perpetuate plants from one season to another.

SCREE BED: An area formed of small stones, together with a few large rocks, usually positioned at the base of a rock garden.

SEED LEAVES: The first leaves that develop on a seedling, which are coarser and more robust than the true leaves.

SEMI-EVERGREEN: A plant that may keep some of its leaves in a reasonably mild winter.

SINK GARDENS: Old stone sinks partly filled with drainage material and then with freely draining compost. They are planted with miniature conifers and bulbs, as well as small rock garden plants. These features are usually displayed on terraces and patios.

SPECIES ROSE: A common term for a wild rose or one of its near relatives.

STAMEN: The male part of a flower.

STANDARD: A tree or shrub trained to form a rounded head of branches at the top of a clear stem.

SUB-SHRUB: Small and spreading shrub with a woody base. It differs from normal shrubs in that when grown in temperate regions its upper stems and shoots die back during winter.

TENDER: A plant which will not tolerate cold conditions is referred to as tender.

TOPSOIL: The uppermost fertile layer of soil that is suitable for plant growth.

TUBER: A swollen, thickened and fleshy stem or root. Some tubers are swollen roots (dahlia), while others are swollen stems (potato). They serve as storage organs and help to perpetuate plants from one season to another.

VARIEGATED: Usually applied to leaves and used to describe a state of having two or more colours.

VARIETY: A naturally occurring variation of a species that retains its characteristics when propagated. The term is often used for cultivars.

WILDLIFE POND: An informal pond, often positioned towards the far end of a garden, which encourages the presence of wildlife such as frogs, birds, insects and small mammals.

INDEX

ACKNOWLEDGEMENTS

t *top* **b** *below* **l** *left* **r** *right* ***Directory a–f***, *starting from top*

Liz Eddison 6, 7, 18t,b, 21, 26, 34r, 36l, 37r, 38r, 42r, 64d, 102c /
Natural & Oriental Water Gardens 40r / Designer: Georgina Steeds 23, 30;
The Garden Picture Library / Geoff Dann 77b / Sunniva Harte 75c, 79b /
J.S Sira 44 / Juliette Wade 22b, 36r;
John Glover 2,4,5, 10-11,12t,b, 14t,b, 15, 16t,b, 20t,b, 22t, 24, 32-33, 34l, 35l,r, 37l,
39l,r 40, 41l,r, 42l, 43r, 48, 50, 51, 55, 57, 58, 60-61 /
Designer: Terry Hill, Hampton Court "99" 1 / Designer: Barbara Hunt 38l /
Designer: Alan Titchmarsh 13, 17, 19;
Lucy Huntington 28;
Peter McHoy 64a,b,c,f, 65a,c,d,e, 66a,b,c,d,e,f, 67a,b,c,d,f, 68a,b,c,e,f, 69c,e,f,
70a-f, 71a,b,d,e,f, 72a-f, 73a,b,c,d,e, 74a,c,d,e,f, 75a,d,e,f, 76b,d, 77c,e, 78b,d,e,f,
79c,d,e, 80c,e, 81b,c,d, 82b,c, 83b,c,e,f, 84a,c,d,e,f, 85a-f, 86a,b,d,e,f, 87a-f,
88a,b,d,e,f, 89c,f, 90a,c,d,e,f, 91a,c,f, 92b,c,d,e, 93a-f, 94b,c,d,e,f, 95a,b,e,f, 96a,c,e,f,
97b,c,d,f, 98a,c,e,f, 99a,b,c,d,e, 100a-f, 101a-f, 102b,d,e,f, 103c,d,e,f, 104a,c,d,e,
105a,b,e,f, 106b,d,e, 107a,e,f;
The Harry Smith Collection 64e, 65b, 67e, 68d, 69a,b,d, 71c, 73f, 74b, 75b, 76a,d,
77a,d,f, 78a,c, 79a,f, 80a,b,d,f, 81e,f, 82d,e,f, 83a,d, 86c, 88c, 89a,b,d,e, 91b,d,e, 92a,f,
94a, 95c,d, 96b,d, 97a, 98b,d, 99f, 102a, 103a,b, 104b,f, 105c,d, 106c,f, 107b,c,d;
David Squire 65f, 76c,f, 81a, 82a, 84b, 90b, 97e, 106a.